YOUNG CHILDREN'S HEALTH AND WELLBEING

SAGE was founded in 1965 by Sara Miller McCune to support the dissemination of usable knowledge by publishing innovative and high-quality research and teaching content. Today, we publish over 900 journals, including those of more than 400 learned societies, more than 800 new books per year, and a growing range of library products including archives, data, case studies, reports, and video. SAGE remains majority-owned by our founder, and after Sara's lifetime will become owned by a charitable trust that secures our continued independence.

Los Angeles | London | New Delhi | Singapore | Washington DC

HELEN CAZALY

YOUNG CHILDREN'S HEALTH AND WELLBEING

FROM BIRTH TO 11

 Learning Matters

Learning Matters
A SAGE Publishing Company

Learning Matters
A SAGE Publishing Company
1 Oliver's Yard
55 City Road
London EC1Y 1SP

SAGE Publications Inc.
2455 Teller Road
Thousand Oaks, California 91320

SAGE Publications India Pvt Ltd
B 1/I 1 Mohan Cooperative Industrial Area
Mathura Road
New Delhi 110 044

SAGE Publications Asia-Pacific Pte Ltd
3 Church Street
#10-04 Samsung Hub
Singapore 049483

Library of Congress Control Number: 2022930445

British Library Cataloguing in Publication Data

A catalogue record for this book is available from the British Library

Editor: Amy Thornton
Senior project editor: Chris Marke
Project management: TNQ Technologies
Marketing manager: Lorna Patkai
Cover design: Wendy Scott
Typeset by: TNQ Technologies
Printed in the UK

ISBN: 978-1-5297-8042-0
ISBN: 978-1-5297-8041-3 (pbk)

At SAGE we take sustainability seriously. Most of our products are printed in the UK using FSC papers and boards. When we print overseas we ensure sustainable papers are used as measured by the PREPS grading system. We undertake an annual audit to monitor our sustainability.

Contents

About the author   vii

Introduction   1

1   Health determinants and causes for concern   9

2   Public health issues and campaigns   20

3   Definitions and measurements of poverty   30

4   Child mental health issues – an escalating concern   43

5   Effective nutrition and children's needs   54

6   The role of media on children's worlds   66

7   Environmental influences   78

8   The impact of physical/genetic conditions   89

Conclusion: what does the future hold?   100

References   107

Index   115

About the author

Helen Cazaly has been a Senior Lecturer at Nottingham Trent University since 2015 delivering across a range of childhood and early years programmes within the Nottingham Institute of Education.

Helen has also been a Trustee for the Professional Association for Childcare and Early Years (PACEY) and is currently an external examiner for the early childhood degree programme at the Pen Green Centre.

Prior to moving to Nottingham Trent University, Helen worked across provision at Truro and Penwith College in Cornwall delivering on a range of FE courses and on degree programmes offered as a Partner College to Plymouth University. She has also provided mentor support for Initial Teacher Training and Early Years Professional Status via the Open University and NDNA partnership.

Before moving to an academic career Helen owned and managed a childcare and early education setting in Cornwall which was graded 'outstanding' by Ofsted.

Introduction

Health is a concept that is often taken for granted in children. As long as a child is physically active, appears well and is succeeding in school, there is an assumption that all is well in their world. The growing statistics of child mental health issues, however, tell a different story, as do the statistics for childhood obesity and physical health issues in childhood which both increase year on year. The over-arching issues of poverty and the ways in which this is measured also impact all other areas of the childhood experience and the inequality of opportunities available to some children. This book aims to explore the main issues that create this escalating situation and which of these are targeted by the UK government as key policy areas with varying levels of success. Underpinning these policy areas and initiatives is the third sector (voluntary ad charity support and non-government organisations) within the United Kingdom and the overarching issues attached to providing the support needed to families at the optimum time to reduce the impact of social inequalities on a child's long-term health outcomes. The book also considers the wider implications of adverse childhood experiences and the geographical issues attached to contemporary childhood experiences, also known as the postcode lottery of childhood. Each area discussed is supported by key recent literature in the form of research and reports as well as both classic and contemporary childhood and other relevant theory to support the analysis of the areas of discussion. Case studies are used in each chapter to give more in-depth examples of the issues under discussion and consider how these issues may manifest in typical family life. An overview of recommended areas of policy focus and health promotion are discussed throughout as well as supportive practice applicable to all areas of the children's sector. Each chapter also provides recom-mended further reading that can support understanding of the issues discussed within the chapter.

Wellbeing is a subjective term that can really only be defined by the person themselves. Our wellbeing can fluctuate from day to day and from hour to hour and children's experience of wellbeing is the same. While there are minor things that can bring these daily changes such as good relationships with friends and family, supportive education professionals and structures as well as a good range of activities to entertain and develop young minds, there are also key areas of a child's life that can have a major impact on their overall health and wellbeing. These areas are called 'health determinants' and a child's access to, and experience of, these determinants can affect their short-term, medium-term and longer-term outcomes in life. There is often a key focus on a child's physical health and development with less awareness and understanding of the needs of a child to have good wellbeing that will contribute to good mental health. The NHS Long Term Plan (2019) clearly states that physical and mental health should have parity of esteem for all health service users, and children are no exception to this approach with government policy working towards a more balanced approach to health promotion and health services that takes into consideration good emotional wellbeing as part of the mental health aspect of the National Health Service.

Despite commitment to a parity of esteem between physical and mental health, there remain a wide range of key issues that prevent some children accessing good quality childhoods with statistics rising year on year of children with issues related to poor nutrition, obesity, poor mental health and families experiencing poverty. Added to this there are a number of other adverse childhood experiences which are known to contribute to poor outcomes to wellbeing and mental health in later adult life. Adverse childhood experiences, commonly referred to by the acronym ACEs, are described by the children and young people's mental health charity, Young Minds as *highly stressful, and potentially traumatic, events or situations that occur during childhood and/or adolescence* (Young Minds, 2018). These events or situations can be experienced either as one-off single happenings or a series of events that threaten the safety and security of a child or young person enough to erode their trust or damage them in other ways. There are many ACEs but some are listed below to give a clear idea of the range and type of events to which ACEs can refer:

- Physical abuse
- Sexual Abuse
- Emotional Abuse
- Living with a person with a drug dependency (including some prescription medications)
- Living with a person with an alcohol dependency
- Witnessing and experiencing domestic violence
- Living with a person who has been in prison
- Living with a person who is experiencing severe mental illness
- Loss of a parent through divorce, death or abandonment

There has been much research in recent years into the impact of ACEs on children's long-term outcomes with clear links shown between the number of ACE experiences in childhood and the risk of the person developing health-harming behaviours themselves in their teens or adult life. These health-harming behaviours can include substance misuse (drugs and alcohol) as well as sexual behaviour. There are also clear links to health outcomes such as cancer, obesity and heart disease in later life and in the much longer term a reduced life expectancy (Hughes et al., 2016). These experiences also demonstrate a higher incidence of mental health issues for the child both in childhood and in later life such as anxiety and depression and post-traumatic stress.

Many children will experience at least one of the events on this list with a possible 9% experiencing four or more (Bellis et al., 2014) with all the potential implications on future outcomes that this figure suggests including a range of risky and risk-taking behaviours that include unintended teenage pregnancies, smoking, binge drinking, drug use and violence. Although the main focus of this book is the health and wellbeing related to young children, it has to be kept in mind that many of the issues that present in older children and teenagers have their roots in a child's early years experiences so awareness of these should be of key importance to those professionals working with the younger age ranges.

The chapters of this book explore a range of health determinants and consider the inter-related nature of them in order to consider the role of government policy in supporting these childhoods and childhood experiences as there is a developing an urgent need to recognise that the families with challenges within the range of health determinants are often the same families that present childhoods that are less than ideal and may contribute to long-term societal concerns in the wider context as well as pressures on both the physical health services and mental health services. Early intervention appears to be key but sometimes, despite effective interventions being available and in place, these families and children are not identified at a stage where mitigations and support can be put in place.

The book is also written in the context of the ongoing global COVID-19 pandemic which has had a major impact on all children and their families with school closures for some (but not all) and lockdowns in place for all families across Britain in the early months of the pandemic. While much of the long-term impact can only be conjecture at this stage, the book uses emerging research throughout to attempt to determine the scale and nature of the issues created alongside the previous existing situation prior to the emergence of the virus.

Chapter 1: Health determinants and causes for concern

In this chapter, the key health determinants are introduced and discussed along-side the main issues related to these areas. The current situation for children is investigated using statistics from before the pandemic and those early statistics emerging as a result of the pandemic. This chapter also considers the role of government in childhood and how they decide priorities within their policy agenda. The role of the Children's Commissioners in all home countries of the United Kingdom is explored alongside the ongoing implementation of children's rights from the United Nations Convention on the Rights of the Child (UNICEF, 1989).

The research explored in this chapter is the theory that underpins a lot of the subsequent chapters, and there is a research focus on Urie Bronfenbrenner's Ecological Systems Theory (1979) as a way of demonstrating how the wider implications of government policy as well as values and attitudes in a society can have a deep and lasting impact on a child's experience of childhood and their future outcomes. A fuller exploration of adverse childhood experiences is included in this chapter alongside considering the role of contemporary childhood and parenting choices and lifestyles. The concept of health promotion is explored with the question investigated as to why people do not have healthy lifestyles. A theme which is developed further in Chapter 2.

Chapter 2: Public health issues and campaigns

Chapter 2 explores current public health issues that have clear campaigns running that can be associated with child health and are supported by government policy. This chapter also introduces the concept of sustainable childhoods and how health promotion can work towards this aspect of child health through support for both children and their families in giving them the knowledge they need to make healthy choices and have healthy lifestyles.

The research focus in this chapter is on health promotion theories. Health pro-motion theory is the theory that supports the creation of health promotion cam-paigns and how they are designed to create awareness and either enhance existing knowledge or counteract the false beliefs some people may have related to health and health choices. The research focus of this chapter also explores how behaviour change can be supported through health promotion and where to aim health promotion resources according to the state of mind or knowledge already existing in the target audience.

The role of the third sector – non-government organisations, voluntary organisa-tions and charities – is explored in this chapter too as a vital form of support for public health education.

Chapter 3: Definitions and measurements of poverty

This chapter explores the issues related to childhoods where the family income is too low to meet all the needs of the family. It explores the different ways of measuring poverty and considers how the government sets a minimum income threshold below which additional support can be put in place. Further exploration of the issues highlights those families missed by the government measurements, and examples are given of how this may manifest in everyday life. The chapter explores working family poverty and how small changes in circumstances can create big issues for financial management and subsequent childhood experience. This leads to a discussion of how effective measurement systems for poverty can be and if alternatives would be better suited to deciding where support should be targeted.

The chapter also considers geographical inequalities – what is known as the 'postcode lottery' of childhood experience and the research focus explores theoretical perspectives on why poverty exists with a discussion of the 'culture of poverty' as well as how the governmental structures and policies can actually create the inequalities in society. The chapter then considers social mobility and the attainment gap between children from more affluent households and those from lower income families. This gap in educational achievement, which had been slowly reducing due to policy interventions, now appears to be widening, rather than continuing to reduce, as a result of the pandemic and the inequality of experience of those families who were already on low incomes. The chapter also begins to consider the interwoven nature of health determinants with particular interest in how poverty, nutrition and mental health can overlap and create more complex situations for children and their families. The case study for this chapter explores how poverty can be experienced in working families, rather than considering poverty from a stereotypical standpoint that it only affects those families in receipt of welfare benefits.

Chapter 4: Child mental health issues – an escalating concern

This chapter explores the incidence of children's mental health issues in all age groups presenting strong evidence that these issues and concerns can be in place from two years old and upwards. It discusses the need for early intervention and practitioner awareness as well as the long-term and ongoing issues with funding mental health services for children and young people. The chapter also explores the stigma attached to mental health and considers how the third sector works together with government policy and interventions to support campaigns to reduce the misinformation and stigma surrounding mental health issues.

The chapter brings recent research into focus with reference to the emerging data from the global COVID-19 pandemic as it relates to British children and considers how the increased numbers of children now experiencing probable mental health conditions can be supported and guided through a system that was already struggling with funding and staffing even before the pandemic started. The case study explores the issues associated with recognition of mental health issues in the early years and proposes that mental health awareness should be a key part of all practitioner awareness and ongoing professional development in order to mitigate the influence of issues as early as possible.

Chapter 5: Effective nutrition and children's needs

This chapter explores how children's nutrition can impact their development and has a particular focus on the issues of poor nutrition including deficiencies and over-nutrition presenting as childhood obesity. It considers the way children's nutritional needs differ from adults and how health promotion campaigns can support parents and the children themselves, to make healthy choices. The effectiveness of the ongoing government strategy of the National Child Measurement Programme is considered alongside other key health campaigns that are designed to support good nutrition in childhood. With childhood obesity rates still going up, the chapter explores why this may be the case despite clear health promotion and policy focus on this area of child health for a number of years.

The overlaps between problematic diets and nutrition and poverty are explored, and the role of interventions based around school meals are investigated. Celebrity influencers and campaigners have had much success in changing government policy and strategies in the field of child nutrition, but there is still more to be done if the statistics for child obesity and deficient diets are to be tackled effectively.

The research focus explores Bronfenbrenner's Ecological Systems Model (1979) with an exploration of both the *microsystem* and its influence as well as the *macrosystem* and wider influences in society. The case study explores this further and considers the overlapping nature of nutrition and family income when making nutritional choices for children.

Chapter 6: The role of media on children's worlds

This chapter explores children's use of media from infanthood and how this may influence healthy development both physically and mentally. The discussion focuses on healthy media use and considers the research that explores how children actually use digital media and the parental attitudes towards this. The chapter explores how prior research has influenced policy and which recommendations have been achieved and which have not in the fast-changing world of the internet and digital media.

The chapter also explores the commercialised nature of childhood and children's experiences and also considers how the media may contribute to sexualised childhoods through the lens of *innocence* versus *knowledge*. There is discussion of government policy through age limits for such things as films and computer games but an exploration of how these may not be working as intended is also discussed. The support available for parents is explored through third-sector organisations and national policy to consider if the measures in place are actually working.

The research focus in this chapter explores the concept of contemporary childhoods being immersed in digital media from the start and what influence this may have on the way the children acquire knowledge and play. The case study explores this further by considering how characters from the media can become woven into all aspects of a child's cultural worlds and considers the potential impact of this on practice and parenting.

Chapter 7: Environmental influences

Chapter 7 builds on the geographical inequalities outlined in Chapter 3 (definitions and measurement of poverty) and explores them in more depth with a focus on how rural and urban childhoods may differ as well as inequality of access to services due to household income levels. The issues related to housing and the cost of living as well as the pollution levels in city childhoods are discussed, and the stereotypes of both rural and urban childhoods are explored. The reality of these childhoods is discussed in order to challenge the stereotypes widely held. Discussion of issues surrounding transport and access to services is included, and the consideration of how this can have an impact on children's social worlds and ability to access extracurricular activities is also investigated.

The chapter also explores wider environmental influences with a focus on the child's *microsystem* (Bronfenbrenner, 1979) and how relationships within the family can contribute to the child experiencing conflict. The case study explores how the changed circumstances of the pandemic can create fractures within a family that had not previously had issues, and the research focus explores a range of studies led by Professor Sir Michael G. Marmot exploring how health inequalities can be insidious in society and how to mitigate them.

Chapter 8: The impact of physical/genetic conditions

Chapter 8 explores how the presence of health conditions within a family can affect a child's experience of childhood. The discussion considers children with physical health conditions and/or genetic conditions and how this can impact the wider family, but the chapter also explores how disability within a family, of any family member can create health inequalities for the entire family. The chapter explores support for parents and siblings as well as considering the issues of young carers, many of whom are not even aware that they are carers. The case study explores these issues in more depth and considers siblings and how these issues may present in education settings and how practitioner awareness can make all the difference to these children.

The chapter also explores how children's education is supported when they have a physical health condition or genetic condition with the role of portage in the early years being explored as a government policy strategy. The role of hospital education to support those children with long-term health conditions is discussed alongside how children are educated when being cared for in the home.

The research focus for this chapter is based around disabled children's experiences throughout the pandemic and how support for these children and their families has been reduced or removed. Families with any disabled member have been disproportionately affected by the pandemic, and the way to support them for the remainder of the pandemic and the recovery period is considered.

Conclusion: What does the future hold?

The Conclusion brings together all the chapters and focuses on the inter-related nature of health determinants and how one cannot be viewed in isolation without considering the others. The interwoven nature of poverty, mental health and nutrition is explored and key areas of health promotion are considered that take into account these overlaps.

The Conclusion goes on to consider how the COVID-19 pandemic has changed the nature of health outcomes for many children, despite children being less likely to suffer badly from the virus itself. It then goes on to consider how future policy commitments are likely to be received and considers the early emerging research that highlights where the need is likely to be greatest to support young children and their families.

Finally, it concludes with key recommendations for practitioners working with young children and their families across the entire children's sector in recognition of the key role they play in early intervention through awareness of how issues materialise and present through a child's infancy and primary school years.

1 Health determinants and causes for concern

Introduction

Childhood is a complex, but relatively short, life stage that has an ongoing impact on the rest of that individual's life experiences. There is often a focus on education and 'training' the child for later adult independence and emotional stability, but in recent years there has been a developing understanding of the role of a range of other influences on a child's outcomes that can contribute to their overall health across their lifetime. These areas of influence are referred to as *health determinants* – those aspects of life that contribute to health outcomes in the short, medium and longer term. Although there are a broad range of health determinants all of which are interwoven and overlap throughout life, there are key areas which have the most dramatic input on a healthy childhood and are of interest throughout this book. When these areas are considered from a child wellbeing perspective they tend to fall into three main areas: experience of poverty, adequate nutrition and mental health issues. These areas then have further contributory factors relating to geographic location and environment; media use; and medical, physical or genetic conditions. All of these combine to become key areas of government focus, or policy, largely due to the statistical evidence that suggests there are major areas of issue and concern in each for children and their families.

Focus on policy

The United Nations Convention on the Rights of the Child (UNICEF, 1989) gave governments clear responsibilities to children in the form of the 54 agreed articles of the convention. These articles were agreed by the United Kingdom in 1990 and brought into force across the United Kingdom in 1992. This has been implemented in Britain by the introduction and revision of legislation and incorporated into key policy agendas that provide support for children and their families. The policy initiatives that stem from this include support such as the benefits system and welfare state with the NHS providing free access to health care for children including dental treatments and eye care as well as the support offered through GP surgeries and hospital treatment if needed. Sadly much of the support intended is overwhelmed by the level of need and many areas of health support are not as accessible as would be ideal. A key example here is dental treatment where access to an NHS dentist is patchy across the country with many families unable to access an NHS service at all (NHS England, 2021) and reports of three-year waiting lists as a result of the COVID-19 pandemic are emerging. This contributes to the concerns of a *postcode lottery* for childhood experience and demonstrates that there is a geographic inequality to many children's lives with many research studies finding that outcomes for children's health are vastly different depending upon which area of the country the child is growing up. Issues related to disadvantage tend to be located in clear pockets within the country as can be seen by the data from the Poor Beginnings study (National Children's Bureau, 2015). This is underpinned by data from studies such as the National Child Measurement Programme which measures and weighs primary school children in their Reception year and then again in Year 6 in order to be able to provide feedback to parents if their child is deviating from the typical weight ranges expected for their age and height. The resulting annual report consistently finds a correlation between children from disadvantaged backgrounds and the issues of being overweight or obese, with little change in recent years despite extensive policy commitments since 2016 to reducing childhood obesity (Department of Health and Social Care, 2020).

Government policy agendas tend to emerge in response to issues. For example, in 2016 the first childhood obesity plan mentioned above (Department of Health and Social Care, 2017) was developed in response to the rising issue of excessive weight in children and young people. Other policies have a broader remit and have their roots in a range of other reports that have been undertaken for the government. An example of this type of policy is the Healthy Child Programme (Department of Health, 2009) which was developed partially in response to the Marmot Review: Fair Society, Healthy Lives (Marmot et al., 2010). Michael Marmot and his team extensively reviewed the lives and outcomes of the people of England and made clear recommendations and suggestions to the Labour government of the time for policy development to improve outcomes. The government response was the Healthy Child Programme (2009) which outlined clearly what care and support children and families could expect to receive and covered pregnancy to 5 years. This was later developed to expand the age range to 19 years with support identified at each stage of childhood. While this is the overarching policy for child health there are many others that run alongside – sometimes specifically targeting children, but often targeting the entire population, with families being one part of the whole.

Who does the policy miss?

Government policy is dynamic. That is to say it flexes and changes according to need but it is safe to say that where there is a need, such as poverty, childhood obesity and children's mental health, a policy will be in place, or in development if it is an emerging need, such as the current position with the aftermath of the pandemic to deal with. Some policy comes about through reviews and reports while others come from statistical data that suggest there is an issue. Whichever way the policy is created, there will always be children and families that are missed for many reasons. To relate this back to a policy initiative already mentioned, the National Child Measurement Programme, the children missed by this are all those not in Reception or Year 6. This clearly includes all early years settings and secondary school age children. While a measurement at age 5 and then again at age 11 is a good indicator of child health for those age groups, it cannot be assumed that all weight-related issues can be captured at these ages, particularly those relating to nutrition deficiencies such as lack of certain vitamins that create health issues or cause a child to be underweight. These can, of course, happen at any point in childhood and not just in Reception year and in Year 6.

A further example of children missed by policy is in the way certain issues are measured. Poverty, for example has a differing measurement by the government than by charities within this field such as the Joseph Rowntree Foundation. This means that the thresholds for support are not necessarily meeting the needs of all the population. The schools attended by children who are entitled to a free school meal due to a low family income are entitled to claim pupil premium, or early years pupil premium, in order to provide additional support for children who are disadvantaged. This system of support relies on parents making a claim for a free school meal or declaring their income status to the setting. All children are entitled to the universal free school meal offer in years Reception, 1 and 2, and there is no reason for parents to declare their income status; so ensuring the children entitled to further support are always identified becomes something of a minefield. This also impacts early years settings and their funding as there are not free meals on offer within the current early years system. This measure does also not include those children of working families who may not earn enough to provide adequately for their family after meeting housing and fuel (heating) costs. This will be explored in more depth in Chapter 3 when we explore poverty as a health determinant.

The NHS Long-Term Plan (2019) made a commitment to a 'parity of esteem' between physical and mental health. While the overarching mental health policy, No Health Without Mental Health (2011), has been in place since 2011 the numbers of children with identified mental health issues or conditions have grown and grown. The latest projected figures suggest that the pandemic has shifted the statistics in the wrong direction with a possible 1 in 6 children now expected to have an identified issue as opposed to the pre-pandemic figures of 1 in 9. Policy is rapidly in development for meeting the mental health needs of these young people but this is amid an ongoing funding and capacity issue that was already being experienced by the Children and Young People's Mental Health Service (CYPMHS) (previously known as the Child and Adolescent Mental Health Service or, more commonly, as CAMHS). This will be explored in more depth in Chapter 4 as mental health issues are explored, but for now, it becomes an example of an acknowledged need for policy intervention that still has capacity and resource issues despite funding being committed and acknowledgement and awareness of the problems at all levels of government.

The role of the children's commissioners

The role of a Children's Commissioner was created as part of the UK commitment to the United Nations Convention on the Rights of the Child (UNCRC) (UNICEF, 1989) and, although it took a number of years to implement, the countries of the United Kingdom (England, Scotland, Wales and Northern Ireland) all now have their own Children's Commissioner. The Offices of the Children's Commissioners are executive, non-departmental public bodies that are funded by the governments of each of the home countries. They have a remit to promote and actively support children's rights, their views and their interests in all policies and decisions that may affect their lives. Part of this role includes extensive recognition that some children are more vulnerable than others which may make it harder for them to make their views known and therefore need particular representation. The Children's Commissioners of the four home countries provide research that supports governments to develop policy for children and families in the areas most needed and they also make recommendations for best practice and campaign for change. Each Commissioner has their own dedicated website, all of which are freely accessible by children, their families and by professionals and may provide students in the childhood and early years sector with additional and up-to-date information about current issues they are studying. There is a particular focus on child health in all its forms by all four Children's Commissioners.

Urie Bronfenbrenner (1917–2005) developed an *Ecological Systems Model* (1979) that suggested that human development was influenced by a range of environmental and societal fields which was a key change for developmental psychology that had not previously considered the outside influences of a society or a child's environment. He continued to develop and add to his model throughout his career with a resulting name change to the *Bioecological Model* in 1994 (Bronfenbrenner and Ceci, 1994).

The key features of his theory were that the child was at the heart of the *nested systems* of society and that child development was not purely biological, which was the prevailing thought at the time he first published. This changed the way people thought about family and education and also about how public policy could have an indirect impact on children's development.

While many texts supporting student understanding of child development theory will focus on the first two *systems* of Bronfenbrenner's theory, the *microsystem* and the *mesosystem*, when considering child health and the role of society and policy to support healthy childhoods it is very important that the further systems are explored too. This theory will be referred to throughout this book as a key theoretical perspective that supports healthy childhood and child wellbeing.

These systems are often presented as a series of concentric circles known as a 'nested structure' with the individual or child at the centre (Figure 1.1):

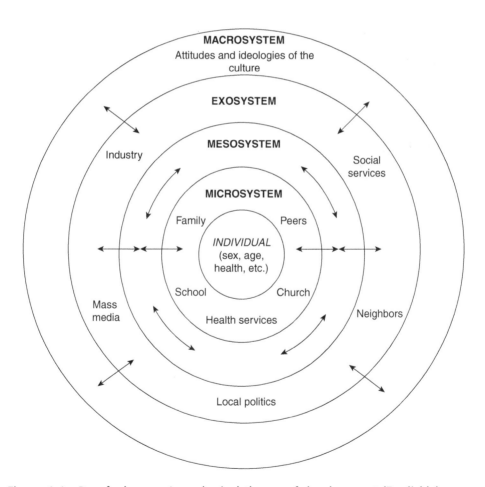

Figure 1.1   Bronfenbrenner's ecological theory of development (English) by Hchokr is licensed with CC BY-SA 3.0

Microsystem

The *microsystem* refers to the people and institutions that are immediate and tangible parts of a child's life. This could be seen as part of the nature/nurture debate where development is influenced by what the child comes in contact with rather than it being a purely biological, sequential pathway of development leading to maturity and adulthood. Examples of typical people who appear in this system and have an influence on the child's everyday lived experiences are shown below:

- Family members such as parents, siblings and grandparents;
- Education professionals such as teachers, teaching assistants and other school staff with close contact;
- Early years professionals such key person and other early years practitioners;
- Children's sector professionals such as health visitors, social workers, audiologist etc;
- Key local religious figures/leaders for those families who follow an organised religion such as a priest, imam or rabbi.

Mesosystem

The *mesosystem* refers to interactions, relating to the child, between the various individuals in the microsystem, for example the communication between a teacher and a parent or between a health visitor and a social worker. These interactions work together to develop knowledge and understanding about the child and therefore contribute to the child's experience. It is important to note here that the *mesosystem* only relates to those interactions rather than the individuals (who already appear in the *microsystem*).

Exosystem

The *exosystem* relates to those places and settings that do not have direct contact with the child but can have a profound influence on their experience of childhood. An example of this would be a parent's place of employment. The child never goes there and the employer does not know the child but the parent's wages have a direct impact on the child as does the hours the parent works and the stress the parent may experience as part of that job role. Also within the exosystem are other areas which have an indirect impact on the child such as the community, media and localised policies or politics from the Local Authority. An example of this would be decisions taken around how much early years funding a setting received, school place allocations or school transport.

Macrosystem

The *macrosystem* is the culture within which the child is growing up. This can be the local culture of a family or religious community but is also the prevailing attitudes and opinions of the country where the child resides. Societal values have large influence within this system and can alter and change over time creating changes to the experience of childhood. The overarching attitudes in the *macrosystem* can influence legislative change and subsequent national policy stemming from this. An example of this would be the development of safeguarding policy and legislation following the shocking death of Victoria Climbié in 2000. The immediate response was the serious case review undertaken by Lord Lamming and published in 2003. This led to the green paper Every Child Matters (2003) which remained in use as practice guidance until 2010 but has now been archived. The Children Act 2004 followed from these which created substantial policy change on the way professionals working with children had to approach information sharing and safeguarding. In this way the *macrosystem* can be seen to be changeable across geographic and time periods – a geo-temporal, dynamic system.

This concept of systems and experiences changing across time is also reflected in the final system, the *chronosystem*, added to the model by Bronfenbrenner in 1994. This system relates to changes and transitions over the life course of the child as well as social circumstances. The COVID-19 pandemic is a current example of how an unexpected event has impacted the life course of children but, equally, the child experiencing a change in family circumstance such as parental divorce could also create a life changing circumstance.

So where does wellbeing fit with health determinants?

Child wellbeing is a subjective position. Although there are many suggested ways of measuring young children's wellbeing such as the Leuven Scales (Laevers, 2005) for those children too young to verbalise their feeling or lacking the communicative ability to do so for other reasons, the end point of measuring wellbeing is always that it is in the opinion of the individual concerned. We know wellbeing can be dynamic from moment to moment across a day depending on what the child is doing, or who they are spending their time with, so we have to consider wellbeing in a broader context and aim for policy and practice that supports all children to develop good emotional wellbeing.

Health determinants are important here as they are key areas where the potential consequences are known to have wide and varying impacts on the child's positive and healthy experience of childhood. This then has an ongoing influence on their subjective wellbeing. For example, a child growing up in a household where money is tight will have an early awareness that their family just cannot afford things that their peers in nursery or school may be able to have and enjoy. This is compounded by the often commercialised nature of British childhood with the continual pressure to own material goods often fuelled by the advertising and marketing industry (Bailey, 2011). This leads children to question why their lives are not running as well as what they see in their friends' experiences (not always perceived correctly) and adds pressure to their family life as they attempt to redress the balance as they see it. We know that there is a connection between low-income families and childhood obesity and we know there are also links between low-income families and diagnosed mental health disorders later in childhood. It is reasonable then to consider that those wider health determinants may have a more direct influence on the child's wellbeing. These are influences that appear in both the *exosystem* and the *macrosystem* of Bronfenbrenner's model (1979) and as such policy agendas attempt to address the issues in order to mitigate the long-term impacts.

How does childhood experience affect adult outcomes?

Much research work and exploration is currently being done around adverse childhood experiences (ACEs) in order to fully understand the potential long-term consequences of some aspects of childhoods in Britain today. ACEs encompass the lived experience of some children and include parental behaviours such as excessive use of alcohol or recreational, illegal drug taking. Also within this is the experience of abuse in all its formats, parents with mental health conditions themselves and growing up in a household where someone is in prison. While there is no direct causal link established between low-income families and children who experience ACEs, there is statistically more incidence of ACEs in areas of high deprivation within Britain.

There are ongoing studies into the long-term impact of ACEs but a recent study found that, compared with people who had not experienced ACEs, adults who had four or more ACEs have a greater risk of developing heart disease; developing type two diabetes; having frequent visits to their GP; have health damaging behaviours such as drinking, smoking and drug use; becoming violent and of going to prison (NHS Health Scotland, 2019). This makes it paramount and abundantly clear that helping children and young people to develop resilience is a constructive way to support those children who will experience adversity in their lives as well as to support their wellbeing throughout childhood. The following case study explores this in more depth.

CASE STUDY – 'IN NEED'

Annie is 4 years old and is in the Reception class at her local primary school. Her mother has been treated for depression since her parents divorced and her older sister has just started secondary school and is finding the transition really hard. The family are living on the mother's wage from a part-time job in the local supermarket that is topped up with universal credit and are in a privately rented house. Annie's teacher has been aware of the family struggling financially as Annie's clothing is all a little too small and her shoes are in poor condition. Annie loves school and engages with her teacher and her peers but the teacher has recently

(Continued)

---

become aware that she has headlice. The standard headlice letter is sent home to all parents in the class, asking them to check their child's hair and treat them if any eggs or lice are found. This raises the awareness of the other children to Annie scratching at her head and become aware of the issue.

Annie's headlice go untreated and the teacher then has a quiet word with Annie's Mum who says she cannot afford nit treatments but she does comb the hair through with a nit comb as often as she can. This situation goes on for several weeks with the headlice being visible in Annie's hair and the other children noticing and starting to tease and call her names. The teacher consults the Designated Safeguarding Lead at the school and they discuss the other issues as well as the headlice such as the poor quality clothes and shoes and that Annie does not always look clean. Eventually the Designated Safeguarding Lead at the school makes a referral to Children's Social Care as they believe that Annie's welfare is at risk and her mum may be in need of support from family support services.

Annie's family is visited by a Children's Social Worker, after a discussion with the teacher and Designated Safeguarding Lead at the school, in order to discuss the situation and they also have a chat with Annie away from her mother, which is best practice as stated by the Working Together to Safeguard Children guidance (2018). This is in line with Section 17 of the Children Act 1989 that requires a multi-agency assessment and should be carried out within 45 days of receiving the referral. When the Children's Social Worker arrives at the house it is very untidy and it is clear that Annie's mum has not been well enough to keep up with the housework as dirty clothes are piled everywhere and food and dirty dishes are left out with mould forming on them. The bathroom is also dirty and there is animal faeces from the family cat in one corner of the lounge. Annie explains to the social worker that they usually get their dinner from the chip shop and sometimes she can have cheese on top of her chips. Her Mum confirms that she has not been able to provide proper meals for a while and that she has been sending the girls to get chips for their tea.

As a result of this assessment the conclusion is that Annie and her sister are 'in Need' but not likely to suffer significant harm and Children's Services draw up a 'Child in Need' plan to support her Mum and help the family get back on track. A 'Child in Need' plan focusses on the support which can be provided to a child and their family. The plan sets out what is already working well and what additional support is needed and why. It specifies which agencies will provide the services and includes what the family and/or the child have agreed to do as well. The plan should have a clear timeframe and reviews should be held at regular intervals.

Annie's GP is contacted and prescribes headlice treatments to deal with the immediate problem and also refers Annie's mum for counselling services.

(Continued)

Children's Services provide help with getting the house clean and tidy and offer ongoing support to help Annie's mum deal with the transition of the older sister into secondary school. Annie's headlice are cleared up and her clothing and footwear improves. The teacher is happy that her concerns have been acted on and that the family is now getting support.

Exploring the case study

This case study demonstrates that sometimes small issues presenting in children are the opening point to see what else is going on in that family. In this case, awareness of the headlice issue led to the class teacher having further concerns about Annie's wellbeing as it was added to the concern around her clothing and footwear. By reporting the issues onwards the family was identified as being in need of support and systems were put in place to support the whole family rather than just providing medications to clear the headlice issue.

How can we advocate for better health practices within families?

Promoting good health practice in families has long been part of the role of everyone working within the children's sector. Teachers promote good education practice such as reading with a child; midwives and health visitors encourage good nutrition with promoting breast feeding to new parents; governments provide additional financial support for the majority of families in the form of child benefit (although this is not available to those families earning in excess of £50,000) as well as a wider benefit system to support those families in most need. An awareness that children need good nutrition is reflected in policy such as the School Food Plan (Dimbleby and Vincent, 2013) that sets out exactly what type and quantity of food should be offered in schools in order that children are getting a fully nutritionally balanced meal as well as the previously mentioned Universal Free School meal offer for children in Reception to Year 2.

Recognition of how much health promotion children's sector professionals actually undertake is not always clear as many roles just take this on as 'part of the job' but it is all health promotion and all aimed to improve children's experiences of childhood and gain better outcomes to take through into adulthood. The question remains as to why the statistics demonstrate that the issues related to the health determinants are just going up and up. Why does all this targeted health promotion not always have the desired results? This will be explored in the next chapter when the role of health promotion in childhood is discussed.

Conclusion

This chapter has introduced the concept of health determinants and has started to explore how aspects of these determinants can overlap each other and have a significant impact on a child's experience of childhood as well as their adult outcomes. Government policy is in place across a wide range of health determinants with initiatives to identify those children who may experience difficulty attaining good health but, despite policy being dynamic and changing according to the needs of the country at the time, there are always children that are missed by the initiatives.

Part of the role of anyone working within the children's sector is that of health promotion. Either directly in their practice with the child or through their work with the wider family. This is not always an acknowledged part of a role but, alongside safeguarding, is inherent in all areas of work with children including in those roles within the third sector or voluntary work with children such as the Scout or Guiding movement. Raising awareness of this aspect of a professional or voluntary role working with children would support practitioners to develop their own knowledge and understanding of the key issues related to health determinants and how to identify families that may need extra support and, potentially, early intervention.

The third sector consisting of charities, voluntary organisations and non-government offices such as the Children's Commissioners are research active and continue to provide a wide range of reports and statistics to enable the policy makers to keep policy dynamic and respond to the needs of the country at the time. Sadly, funding these initiatives can often be the sticking point and governments have to decide where to target their financial support in order for as many children and families to be supported as possible. This will be explored in further chapters related to the health determinants of poverty, nutrition and mental health.

The current circumstances of the country being mid-pandemic has given rise to a fresh set of issues that government policy will need to address in order to mitigate as much as possible the ongoing, as well as long-term, impact on children that the unprecedented situation within which the world has found itself has created. While much health promotion campaigning since March 2020 has focussed entirely on reducing the transmission of COVID-19, the campaigns are now starting to be developed to support the country's recovery and the *catch up* agenda for school age children. Within this framing, it will fall to the professionals working with children and families whose children are not yet in the education system to clearly outline the health needs of these families so that they are also supported and children's ongoing experiences of childhood have an emphasis on reducing the impact of the pandemic.

Recommended further reading

NHS Health Scotland (2019) Adverse childhood experiences in context. Available online at: http://www.healthscotland.scot/media/2676/adverse-childhood-experiences-in-context-aug2019-english.pdf

2 Public health issues and campaigns

- To explore the role of public health campaigns to support improving child health outcomes

- To discover how public health issues can be supported by professionals within the children's sector

- To consider the role of policy to support child health

- To investigate the effectiveness of public health campaigns

- To recognise the role the third sector contributes to public health campaigns

Introduction

Public health has never been closer to the forefront of people's awareness than since the outbreak of COVID-19 and the subsequent issues related to a global pandemic. Public health campaigns for handwashing, face coverings, social distancing, testing and vaccination have never been so evident in everyday life. Health promotion from the National Health Service (NHS) and the government has been clearly on the agenda to prevent the spread and impact of the pandemic. The success of the campaigns however have built on knowledge and understanding of how to promote good and healthy behaviours which have been inherent across all age groups and walks of life for many years. Since the inception of the welfare state and NHS in 1948, providing information and support to prevent health issues has been one of the key areas of effort in order to improve the nation's health and not create too much of an expensive, or excessive, demand on the health service providers. This was dramatically obvious near the start of the pandemic with the government key health message slogan at the start of the first lockdown in March 2020 – *Stay Home, Protect the NHS, Save Lives*. The message slogan used here was not just to stop people catching and passing on the virus but was a clear call to prevent the NHS from being overwhelmed by too many people needing care at the same time. This was, and remains, a key feature of health promotion during the management of the pandemic but it has its roots in health promotion strategies that are preventative in order to avoid undue pressure on NHS services.

How the NHS promotes healthy lifestyles and choices

Within the NHS, areas of health promotion such as childhood vaccinations and screenings are all designed to either prevent disease or to provide early identification of issues in order to attempt to reduce the escalation of some conditions as well as to have clear management of others (e.g. screening for conditions such as Down's syndrome, autism spectrum or speech and language issues).

Government policy agendas have been directed towards public health promotion for children and families for a number of years now with regular government commissioned reviews feeding into updates and support for children and families according to the needs outlined by the resulting reports. Key reviews are those such as the Marmot Review – Fair Society, Healthy Lives (Marmot et al., 2010) that supported the development of the Healthy Child Programme 0–5 years (2009) which outlines exactly what support and screening should be available to all children and families in England. Another key review leading to policy development was the Field Review, The Foundation Years (Field, 2010), that explored the issues related to poverty in the United Kingdom and whose findings contributed to changes to the welfare benefit system to provide support for low income families. Reviews contributing to policy development and reform are an essential component of public health promotion in order to know that the support being developed is being targeted towards the families that need it the most. The success of this is not always assured, however, as rising statistics for poverty and childhood obesity will clearly outline, but in other areas such as child vaccinations there are clear successes, with incidence of childhood diseases, that are routinely vaccinated against, having reduced to such as extent that they are now considered a rarity rather than a typical childhood illness.

The role of public health in supporting sustainable childhoods

> *The foundations for virtually every aspect of human development, including physical, intellectual and emotional, are established in early childhood. Sustaining this across the life course for school-aged children and young people is important to improve outcomes and reduce inequalities through universal provision and personalised response. There may be challenges within a child's or a young person's life and times when they need additional support.*

(No Child Left Behind, Public Health England, 2020)

Quite often when we hear or use the word 'sustainable' we immediately think of the environment and issues related to recycling or climate change. Sustainability also refers to people and society being able to maintain themselves throughout their life course and is explored in more depth in Chapter 7 when we look at environmental issues affecting healthy childhoods. Sustainability, when considered in the context of childhood, relates to children's experience of childhood enabling them to go on to lead healthy, productive adult lives with the ability to form good relationships; gain employment that supports them in good housing with a good lifestyle attached and to have community development where people feel a part of society and to be able to contribute, via National Insurance contributions and a pension scheme, to support systems to maintain themselves throughout their life course. If a society can create sustainable childhoods, then the financial and social impact is reduced when those children become adults. Health promotion is an integral part of developing sustainable childhoods as health behaviours and decisions taken during childhood can have a lasting impact throughout the lifespan of a person. National policy, such as the Healthy Child Programme 0–19 (2009), provides a clear outline of ways that families and children should have support at different stages in order that those children should grow and develop in a sustainable way to the society of which they are a part. The Healthy Child Programme has been in use in varying formats since 2009 and has reviews and updates regularly to modernise the programme with the recent published implementation guidance, *Best start in life and beyond*, stating the goal is *to ensure that every child gets the good start they need to lay the foundations of a healthy life* (Public Health England, 2021).

Why don't people make healthy choices?

One of the most complex parts of human behaviour to understand is why people do not make healthy choices for themselves or for their children. This has been a main focus for theorists exploring health and risk behaviours, and their work contributes to the growing understanding we have of health behaviours. This is important because when health promotion materials are designed it is really important that the right audience is targeted as well as providing the information that will help them to alter their behaviours. The main way this is done is by considering what the person's 'health beliefs' are as a starting point. If someone's current belief and knowledge can be explored, then health promotion materials can focus on key areas that will support new knowledge and understanding and encourage the individual to change their behaviours.

WHAT DOES THE RESEARCH TELL US?

This concept of a *health belief model* was first suggested in the United States in 1952 as a way of predicting people's health behaviours (Hochbaum et al., 1952). The model suggests that a person will be motivated to behave in a certain way based on three categories: Individual perceptions; modifying factors and the like-lihood of action.

Individual perceptions are the person's own beliefs about the severity and risk of the condition or illness and whether or not they feel they are susceptible to it. A recent example of this would be during the pandemic that older people have been repeatedly told that their risk from COVID-19 of hospitalisation or death is higher and therefore when the request for them to shield at the start of the pandemic came the vast majority of them complied and stayed at home, not seeing family and grandchildren for many weeks, despite how difficult this was for many.

Modifying factors are those factors such as age (using the previous example) that influence the understanding of the possible consequences of a behaviour and of the personal perception of how vulnerable the person may be to the illness or condition.

The likelihood of action in this model is the person's understanding of the potential benefits of taking action minus any barriers that they feel there are to that change in behaviour being made. This combination creates the likelihood of the behaviour change occurring. So in the previous example, an older lady who cares for her grandchildren while their parents work may have considered that the barrier to her 'shielding' was her caring role in the family. To encourage her to change that belief she would have to consider that the risk of hospitalisation or death was very relevant to her, her location and her lifestyle, before seeking alternative types of care being provided for her grandchildren to enable her to 'shield' as requested by the government.

So health belief models explore the potential for people to take preventative action if they believe that there is a personal health risk to themselves or for parents, to their children. These models are based on the assumption that people fear disease and that health behaviour is influenced by the degree of fear that they have of that disease. The more fear they have, the more motivation they have to adapt their behaviours.

Glanz et al. (2002) went on to explore and develop a health belief model in more depth with more of a focus on the *modifying factors* that influenced the perceived susceptibility or the perceived threat or severity. This model then considers that these modifying factors will influence the beliefs about the barriers to changing behaviour. Health promotions should therefore use the *modifying factors* as their core when considering what information is needed for a target audience to make changes. The modifying factors in Glanz's model (2002) are age, sex, ethnicity, personality, socio-economics and knowledge with an extra layer included that suggests there are *cues to action* such as education, symptoms and media infor-mation that will encourage people to make changes. In the case of the previous example of the request for older people to 'shield' there may also be *cues to action* such as intense media attention and government slogans such as *Stay Home, Protect the NHS, Save Lives* as well as seeing figures of positive cases and hospi-talisations rising or experiencing symptoms, either for themselves or from a family member, such as a grandchild, developing a cough or other symptoms that could suggest a COVID-19 infection.

Further research has also been undertaken into understanding how to maintain and sustain changed behaviours.

DiClemente and Prochaska (1998) explored individuals who were attempting to stop addictive behaviours, such as smoking. Although it was developed to support changing addictive behaviours, it is used in health promotion to understand how to initiate behaviour change at the right moment. They proposed a three-stage model of change that includes the *stages of change*, the *processes of change* and the *levels of change*. This is often depicted as a cycle similar to Figure 2.1 below:

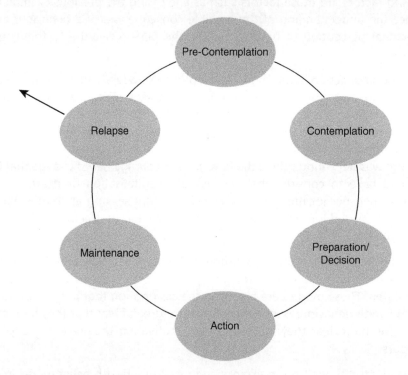

Figure 2.1   Model of change

This model suggests that there is a clear thinking or *contemplation* stage that breaks down to *pre-contemplation* and *contemplation*. Pre-contemplation is when people start to realise that they should be thinking about the issue, and contemplation is more actively thinking about the issue. Many health promotion materials are targeted at these stages by providing knowledge and information for people to be able to move to the next stage. The *processes of change* stage involves preparation for making change and decisions to make that change which moves the individual on to taking action to adapt their behaviours. Once the thinking stage is passed then individuals will go through a decision-making and preparation stage before moving forward to the *action* stage where the new, changed behaviours are instigated. This model also allows for a *relapse* zone where people may discontinue the changed behaviour but, as it is in a cycle, they are able to re-join the cycle and reinstate the changes they had previously been undertaking.

Health promotion to instigate changes in health behaviours are further explored in the case study for this chapter that considers effective health promotion campaigns.

CASE STUDY – MMR

Cassie has a 12-month-old daughter and has been sent a vaccination reminder card for the Measles, Mumps and Rubella (MMR) vaccination from her local GP surgery. She has a chat with her mother who says she thinks there is something about autism being connected to the MMR vaccination and that when Cassie was little many people were choosing not to get their children vaccinated. Cassie makes a note to discuss this with her health visitor next time she attends the drop-in baby clinic in her village.

Exploring the case study

The MMR vaccine protects against three serious illnesses (measles, mumps and rubella) and is part of the UK child immunisation programme, which can be explored further in the suggested further reading for this chapter, *Health Matters: giving every child the best start in life* (Public Health England, 2016). The MMR vaccination is in two parts – the first dose is at 12 months and the second at around 3 years and 4 months old. It is important children receive both doses in order to be fully vaccinated.

The reason Cassie's mother remembered that there was some controversy about the MMR vaccine goes back to 1998 when a research paper was published in the *Lancet* that claimed there was a link between the MMR vaccine and children developing autism. This was then studied extensively by other researchers but no link was found by any other study. In 2004, the *Lancet* stated that it should not have published the original study and formally retracted the study in 2010. The lead author of the study, Andrew Wakefield, was banned from practicing medicine by the British General Medical Council in May 2010. The matter concluded with the *British Medical Journal* fully investigating in 2011 and presenting evidence that the original claim had stemmed from research fraud. What was left, however, was the *urban myth* that the MMR injection caused autism. This had created a mass panic and MMR vaccination rates in Britain dropped dramatically which left an opening for diseases such as measles that had been virtually eliminated prior to this, to take hold again in the United Kingdom. The legacy of this time is that there is still a misconception around the safety of the MMR which can prevent full take up of it by some new parents.

If this case study is explored using the health belief model (Glanz et al., 2002) we can consider that the *modifying factors* here are Cassie's age as she was a child when the controversy happened, so her mother has a memory of the concerns which contributes to the *modifying factor* of knowledge – in this case inaccurate knowledge – that will contribute to Cassie's decisions around whether to take her daughter for the MMR first dose.

Cassie has a long discussion with her health visitor when she attends the baby clinic which is provided by her GP surgery as part of the Healthy Child Programme. The health visitor explains the history and gives Cassie some leaflets and web links to explore the diseases and the vaccine further. Cassie looks at all the material and shares it with her mother, and they both realise that having the MMR vaccination is safe, and the risk of disease is far worse than potential reactions to the injection. Cassie contacts her GP surgery to make an appointment for the first dose for her daughter.

If we apply the *Change model* (DiClemente and Prochaska, 1998) here it can been seen that Cassie visited the health visitor in the *contemplation* stage, having entered the *pre-contemplation* stage when the vaccination reminder card arrived. The health visitor provided information that supported Cassie to enter the *preparation/decision* stage, and she then entered the *action* stage as she made the appointment for her daughter. This also can be related back to the *health belief model* (Glanz et al., 2002) as the information leaflets and web links provided by the health visitor created accurate knowledge for Cassie and her mother which then provided the *cues to action* needed to alter their health beliefs and adapt their behaviours.

Supporting parents to make healthy choices

As can be seen by the case study above, parents often revert to their own parents or family for advice about raising their children or about parenting choices. The role of a supportive family is really important to healthy parenting but sometimes the previous generation do not have the accurate information that the younger parent needs to make informed decisions around parenting issues. This case study used the example of childhood immunisations but there are a significant number of other health choices that parents will make from the decision to breastfeed, nutrition through childhood, schooling, exercise and the choice of ways to discipline to name just a few. Many government-funded health promotion campaigns aim to give parents the up-to-date and accurate knowledge that they need to make informed choices. Many of these campaigns are very well known through the health promotion being effective and the messaging being clear. An example of this would be those that include slogans such as *Breast is Best* to support new parents to choose breastfeeding over bottle feeding, or the *5 a Day* campaign with its clear message that the best nutrition involves including five pieces of fruit and vegetables a day and is part of the wider Change4Life public health campaign. The Healthy Child Programme (2009) states that parents should be provided with information in a range of formats, including digital formats, to support them in developing knowledge before they make decisions so many health campaigns fall under this remit and are funded by the government accordingly – Change4Life being an example of a long-running public health campaign that is run with government funding.

Many of the health issues related to childhood are escalating and the current environment created by the global pandemic will continue long into the recovery period for Britain. Issues such as poverty have been exacerbated and ongoing issues with children experiencing poor mental health are already showing with statistics of children with a probable mental health issues having shifted from one in nine to one in six children (Thandi, 2020a, 2020b). The ongoing battle against childhood obesity will also continue as children who have not been able to attend sports clubs and other extra-curricular activities may not have been able to have the correct energy balance in their lives of calories (food) in and energy (activity) out. These issues will be explored in more depth in the following Chapters 4 and 5 that consider the role of mental health and nutrition as health determinants.

Health promotion and parenting

Health promotion campaigns are very much set in the moment according to the needs of each part of Britain and are led by statistical evidence to identify where there is a need for a policy agenda and a health promotion campaign. Some of these are clearly linked to health such as those relating to weight, nutrition and healthcare but others are somewhat more obliquely linked to child health issues and relate to good parenting techniques that then support the child to have a supportive family environment that helps maintain good wellbeing. Areas of health promotion in this field may include parenting classes or activities run by a school, such as how to support a child's homework effectively. The key message here is that in order for parents to be supported to make the choices and deci-sions related to their children they need to have clear and accurate information about issues available to them at a relevant period in the child's life. One of the main reasons health promotions are not effective is that the information is not relevant or accessible – after all, people may not know they need the information so do not go looking for it. This is a key criticism of the Change4Life campaign in so much as it is mainly run in online formats so a person needs to have already entered that *contemplation* stage of the Change model (DiClemente and Pro-chaska, 1998) in order to know that they need to take action. Posters, online adverts on social media, leaflets and television advertising are all ways to raise awareness of issues and inform parents that this is something they need to think about and explore in more depth and the provision of this information to set the Change model *pre-contemplation* stage running is a key part of all health pro-motion. This is often supported by the third sector, or charities, as awareness raising and support is expensive and cannot always be made available through government funding.

The role of the third sector in health promotion campaigns

When we refer to the *third sector* we mean those organisations that are neither in the public sector nor in the private sector. They are usually independent of the government, although some may receive some of their funding via government departments. This sector can also be known as the *voluntary sector*, the *independent sector* or the *civic sector*. They are quite often a registered charity but not always. Third sector organisations are value-driven and non-profit making. Any funds raised are used to invest in social, environmental or cultural causes including research studies and, in some cases, direct support for families.

Funding for organisations in the third sector can be through government departments or bodies but money is also raised via the general public through donations or charity shop sales and sponsored activities, as popular examples. Larger fundraising bodies such as the National Lottery also distribute funds. All funding received in the third sector goes towards the cause involved or to the running of the operation. This means that research carried out by the third sector is unbiased and can often give a clearer picture of the situation of particular issues at that time. The government welcomes this research and recommendations resulting from it, and uses this to inform their own policy agenda and spending priorities.

When considering the role of the third sector in public health promotion there are a wide range of organisations and charities that provide support and information for causes related to children and childhood health issues. These can range from awareness campaigns such as the NSPCC *Full Stop* campaign to raise awareness of child abuse issues to more targeted campaigns such as Tommy's providing support for baby loss in pregnancy and researching the causes and treatments of pregnancy loss.

Many charities focus their research on understanding the children's perspectives on their worlds such as the Good Childhood Report series (The Children's Society, 2006–2021) that explore children's subjective wellbeing and trends in how children feel about current issues and events in their lives so that campaigns for social change can be targeted at the issues that matter most to the children.

In this way, the third sector has an important role to play in public health campaigns related to children, childhood and families. Not only through the support each organisation is able to provide directly to children and families but in their role as unbiased and independent researchers. The role of the third sector will be referred to throughout the remaining chapters of this book as each area of interest is addressed as these organisations are a key part of the understanding of issues through their research agendas as well as sources of support offered directly to children and their families.

Conclusion

This chapter has explored the role of public health campaigns in creating sustainable and healthy childhoods. The importance of understanding and using health promotion theory has been discussed in order that campaigns created provide relevant information to the target audience that will effect change. The research undertaken by the third sector, or through government commissioned reviews, provides that range of information needed in order to design an effective campaign either within the third sector or through government departments, policy agendas and funding streams. The combination of the role of these agencies that exist within the *macrosystem* work together to make change that directly affects the child at the heart of the *Ecological Systems Model* (Bronfenbrenner, 1979).

As mentioned in the previous chapter, health promotion becomes part of the role of all professionals working with children and their families regardless of in which part of the children's sector their role is maintained. Developing an awareness and understanding of key health determinants and of the ways healthy choices can be effectively promoted to children themselves, as well as to their families, can make a significant difference to the outcomes of individual children. Government policy and initiatives alone are not enough to create clear pathways of knowledge for parents to make decisions, and practitioners are often considered to be key sources of information and support to help those decisions being taken in an informed and sustainable manner.

Recommended further reading

Public Health England (2016). Health Matters: Giving every child the best start in life. Available online at: https://www.gov.uk/government/publications/health-matters-giving-every-child-the-best-start-in-life/health-matters-giving-every-child-the-best-start-in-life

3   Definitions and measurements of poverty

- Understand the impact of poverty on a child's health in general and in some specific areas

- Recognise the different ways that poverty can be measured

- Explore how the way poverty is measured can affect the support a family can receive

- Consider current research findings and data relating to child poverty

- Consider how the effects of poverty are mitigated by government through policy

Introduction

As we have already explored in the preceding chapters, health and wellbeing for children are complex concepts that can be affected by a wide range of issues. When considering poverty as a health determinant, these various other factors have a heavy input into the child's experience of childhood, and moving forward into their adult life these factors still have an enormous and lasting influence on their life course and experience. This chapter will explore some of those key factors such as individual lifestyle; family and genetic issues; social factors as well as environmental influences. Throughout this chapter there will be reference to the wider family of the child, their *microsystem* (Bronfenbrenner, 1979), as it cannot be forgotten, or ignored, that children and young people's lives are affected by the health and wellbeing of those who care for them as well as their own.

One of the key health inequalities experienced in Britain today is the different levels of exposure to risks associated with a child and their family's socio-economic position. Extensive research into this has led by Barnardos, a child health charity that supports children who are vulnerable because they are 'cared for' by the state. The expression *cared for* refers to those children for whom the *Parental Responsibility* is not with their birth parents but, for numerous reasons, has been taken over by the Local Authority where they reside. *Parental Responsibility* is defined in the Children Act (1989) as those rights, duties, powers, responsibility and authority that parents have regarding their child and their property. There is emphasis on responsibility to children rather than rights over children. In some cases *Parental Responsibility* is removed from a parent. This could be because the child's birth parents cannot temporarily provide appropriate care or due to the death of parents as well as those children who have been removed from the care of their birth family. Adopted children are not classified as *cared for*, whereas children in foster care are. Barnardo's overall findings relate to all children, not just *cared for* children, and their 2003 study, led by Duffy and McNeish, explored the strong links to the area that children are growing up in as well as their gender and their ethnicity to consider what impact these socio-economic risks can have (Duffy and McNeish, 2003). It is a sad fact that socio-economic status can be directly linked to health outcomes and life expectancy with factors such as location, environment, income and education playing a key part (WHO, 2017). Put simply, the more affluent an individual or a family is, the more likely they are to have better health (Marmot, 2004).

How can poverty affect childhood?

Poverty during childhood can lead to potentially longer lasting and more severe detrimental outcomes, with impacts carried through to adulthood, creating health conditions including higher rates of depression, respiratory diseases, high blood pressure and arthritis (Tucker, 2018). Children's experience of poverty is a family issue and therefore cannot be viewed in isolation of the rest of the family and circumstances. The *microsystem* and the *macrosystem* (Bronfenbrenner, 1979) combine to create the family's experience of poverty and any support systems in place within society. The ongoing issues for children experiencing poverty include obesity in childhood (NHS Digital, 2021) and a higher incidence of mental health issues (Thandi, 2020a, 2020b), both of which will be discussed in greater depth in Chapters 4 and 5. The Child Poverty Action Group has also found that children living in low income housing are also two and a half times more likely to experience chronic illnesses compared with children living in households that have a family income in excess of £52,000 a year (CPAG, 2021).

In 2010 Frank Field was commissioned by the government of the time to explore the extent and impact of child poverty at the time. The resulting report, *The Foundation Years*, is also commonly known as the *Field Review*, and had a stark message about the impact of child poverty on our society. Field found that poor families were more likely to have infant mortality and that children from those families were more likely to grow up to experience poverty in their adult lives. Alongside these findings were issues related to their behaviour and education with a clear message throughout suggesting that even as young as pre-school, children from poor families are more likely to have conduct disorders and as teenagers are more likely to experience bullying or engage in risky behaviours such as smoking and drinking which, in turn, have long-term health impacts. This has been more recently supported by the findings of a study into the extent of mental health issues that included children of two to four years old (NHS Digital, 2018). Educationally, children from poor families are less likely to achieve well at school and less likely to stay on in education after the age of 16 (the minimum school-leaving age at the time of the report in 2010).

These facts combined gave the Coalition Government of the time a clear message that family income and social class, over which a child has no control, are the greatest predictors of a child's development trajectory and eventual adult outcomes. The recommendations made in the report were that policy was developed with an aim to tackle the root causes of poverty rather than just providing an adequate income via the welfare benefit and tax credit systems. However, as can be seen by the more recent statistics published by the Joseph Rowntree Foundation (2021), child poverty has been steadily increasing rather than decreasing, and the impact of the pandemic has exacerbated the situation for many children and their families far beyond the reach of current policy initiatives to be able to support them.

Definitions of poverty

So what is poverty? Definitions of poverty really matter as they set the basic standards in a society by which we measure who is entitled to additional support and assistance. They set a minimum standard of living and draw a clear line between what we consider, as a society, to be acceptable or unfair. Once a society has defined what poverty means to that particular society the government is able to set policy and develop initiatives to target their support to where their definition indicates the need is greatest. The societal issues arise when the way poverty is measured does not encompass all the families that have financial difficulties within their lives or where the line is drawn for support does not take into consideration key spending the family cannot reduce or avoid.

There used to be two main definitions of poverty – *absolute* and *relative*:

- *Absolute poverty* is the most common way poverty is described. It is entirely based on income levels, and a person is considered 'poor' if their income falls below the minimum level set within their society. This minimum level is set to reflect the basic needs of that society and is usually referred to as the *poverty line*. Support and help are only available to those people whose income falls below that line.

- *Relative poverty* is defined somewhat differently and is based on a person's material needs and circumstances. A person is considered to live in relative poverty when they do not have enough income to take part in activities that are considered an accepted part of daily life in the society in which they live.

However, in more recent years a third definition has been developed to reflect current societal concerns, which is that of *social exclusion*. This is the definition adopted by many of the third sector organisations who conduct research and provide statistics that contrast starkly with the government's own measurement system.

In the United Kingdom, the government conducts and publishes a survey of households below average income annually. This serves the purpose of setting the 'poverty line' in the United Kingdom at 60% of the median national income of a household. The *median* is the middle number in an ascending or descending list of numbers, in this case, household incomes. In the United Kingdom this figure is used to decide who is entitled to help and support via the welfare state, or benefits system. For the purposes of definitions in the United Kingdom this figure is classed as *relative poverty* and currently stands at around 14 million people. The UK definition of absolute poverty, however, uses the same basic measurement system but the key difference is that the line is set at 60% of the national income in 2011.

Measurements and indicators of poverty

In the United Kingdom the annual Family Resources Survey, conducted and published by the Department for Work and Pensions, collects information about a range of households in the United Kingdom using a set of *essential items* as a measurement point. These are known as the material deprivation items and services, and household responses are categorised by those who can afford them, those who would like them but cannot afford them and those who do not want or need the item or to whom this does not apply. Items include such areas as being able to keep up with bills and any debt payment and there are separate items for children such as whether they are able to eat fresh fruit and vegetables each day and whether they have a warm winter coat. There are also items which lean very much towards the *relative poverty* definition, such as whether or not a child is able to attend organised activities outside of school each week. So, although relative poverty could be considered as a subjective measure, there are clear ways of measuring this that are in use by the Department for Work and Pensions, and this annual survey is also used to inform policy decisions and strategies.

The various third sector organisations that work towards a reduction in poverty in the United Kingdom have concerns about the way the government measures poverty as this is what is used to decide entitlements to support such as Universal Credit or free school meals for children beyond Year 2 in Primary School. One of the biggest concerns is that housing and childcare costs are not taken into consideration when setting the poverty line. These are not payments that are optional for a working family and so organisations such as the Joseph Rowntree Foundation discount these from their measurements in their annual review of poverty in the United Kingdom. Their most recent review, using these measures, found that the number of children in the United Kingdom living in poverty was 4.2 million for their 2018–2019 annual report. The report for 2020–2021 was published mid-pandemic and reflected the vast changes that were happening in the United Kingdom at that time. The report for 2021–2022 is hoped to have a more reliable measure of the impact of the pandemic on child poverty (JRF, 2021).

Why does poverty persist and what causes it?

One of the biggest theoretical questions of our time is 'why does poverty persist and what causes it?' If we consider this from a simple standpoint, when poverty is measured as 60% of less than median national income there will always be a proportion of the population that fall below that poverty line because of the use of the median. When we consider that the *median* is the middle number in an ascending or descending list of numbers, if a poverty line is set at below 60% of this *median*, there will always be numerous people below this line. This is *relative poverty* and is considered a justified measure as it explains the experience of poverty as compared with others in the same society. The income figure in use in the United Kingdom would not, for example, be relevant in a developing world country where that same annual income would be seen as affluent relative to others within that particular society.

Therefore, theories have developed to attempt to understand why some people are in that lower strata of income bracket rather than to consider it as an inevitable mathematical conclusion. Theories tend to fall within two main areas – *individual poverty* and *structural poverty*.

Individual poverty

Individual poverty theories stem from a belief that poverty is related to a person's own choices and behaviours. The Poor Laws of the 1830s reflected this belief and considered that poverty in society was necessary in order to motivate people to work and that 'pauperism' (what we would refer to as absolute poverty today) was brought about by '...individual weakness of character – drunkenness, improvidence and fecklessness' (Townsend, 1979). This idea is perpetuated by today's right wing press and political parties with an ongoing suggestion that people using the welfare benefits could change their situation and could avoid poverty by going to work rather than claiming benefits. Policies are developed that support this theory to make work more viable such as working tax credits and childcare tax credit to support people into the workplace and lift them above the income threshold for Universal Credit and other welfare benefits. One of the biggest critiques of this theory is that, in the United Kingdom today, the contrasting figures of families living in poverty by government measures and by third sector measures, such as the End Poverty Coalition or the Joseph Rowntree Foundation demonstrate that *in work* poverty is persistent and contributing to the 4.2 million children who are experiencing a childhood in poverty. *In work* poverty refers to those families where the adults are working but there is still not enough household income to meet the needs of the family.

WHAT DOES THE RESEARCH TELL US?

Closely aligned to this *individual poverty* theory, Oscar Lewis (1914–1970) outlined a theory of a *culture of poverty* (Lewis, 1966) following studies of family life in poor urban areas. He found that there were a range of over 50 traits that over 20% people living in poverty displayed that led to a cross-generational expectation and subsequent experience of poverty. He called this the *culture of poverty* and theorised that children born into poor households grow up with the expectation of being a poor adult and make their life choices accordingly.

Structural poverty

Structural poverty theories, however, attempt to explain the persistence of poverty in developed societies through explanations that the way the society is structured creates the income divides and resulting poor families. Structural inequalities that come from social classes, institutional gender and ethnic discriminations mean that certain members of a society such as women, people from black and minority ethnic (BAME) backgrounds and the lower working classes do not benefit from macro-economic policies introduced in a society and are therefore more likely to experience poverty within their lifetimes. Women with children, for example, still tend to be employed in roles which fit around school hours or, alternatively, the family has additional costs for childcare to enable them to work 'office hours'. This is exacerbated for a lone parent, of either gender, who has all the same expenses as a settled couple but with the limitations of having school age children and their additional need for care out of school hours. While government policy attempts to address this through provisions such as extended schools offering before and after school care and childcare tax credits to support those families with children not yet of school age, the situation remains that is a more costly and complex process for those families to access well-paid, full-time employment. The ongoing divide between male and female salaries and BAME salaries compared with White British workers are demonstrated by the annual figures reported to government in the gender pay gap report. This demonstrates that this discrepancy is a current and relevant cause of concern with a gender pay gap of 15.5% (ONS, 2020) and an ethnicity pay gap that varies widely according to ethnic background but is reported to be as high as 16% for those workers of Pakistani ethnic backgrounds (ONS, 2019).

The government policy position

Regardless of how poverty is measured or where the poverty line is set, the government has to create policy that mitigates the impact of poverty on children and families. Part of the United Nations Convention on the Rights of the Child (UNICEF, 1989) gives a clear government responsibility to create a support structure in societies for children and families. In Britain this is done through a variety of ways but the main systems of support remain the welfare benefit system (Universal Credit) and tax credits systems supplemented by such policies as the free school meal offer for children in Year 3 upwards for low-income families and the 15 hours a week nursery place offer for disadvantaged two-year-olds. This policy position veers towards viewing the route out of poverty as being through education for children and work for parents with working parents of three- and four-year-olds being able to claim an additional 15 hours a week in an Early Years setting on top of the standard 15-hour nursery education to which all three- and four-year-olds are entitled. It is worth pointing out, however, that 30 hours provision is only for 39 weeks of the year (or 525 hours annually) so there is an onus on the full-time working parent to either pay for supplementary provision or to rely on family and friends during the other weeks of the year when a nursery place is not available. This means that despite policy being in place that is intended to support that family into the workplace, there is still a gap in the support that the family themselves must fill.

The universal free school meal offer is in place for all children in Reception, Year 1 and Year 2 but becomes means tested from Year 3 onwards. In line with the differing measures of poverty, the means testing does not take into consideration working family poverty, with the maximum income a family can receive being £7,400 (after tax) to be eligible. This means that one million children who live below the UK poverty line are not eligible for a free school meal beyond Year 2 (CPAG, 2021) thereby creating an ineffective sole strategy solution for poor nutrition in low income families. There are also major gaps in the provision for those children who are entitled, with weekends and holidays not being included in the offer. This has received a lot of attention throughout the pandemic with footballer Marcus Rashford leading a campaign for food vouchers to be given to those families who were not able to attend schools in lockdown and then to extend the free school meal offer to holiday periods. The government did agree to the main holiday periods but not to half term weeks and not as an ongoing adaptation as we move out of the pandemic and back towards a more normal way of life. This example of the power of a campaign demonstrates the role of the *macrosystem* (Bronfenbrenner, 1979) in society that was explored as the research focus in chapter one, as the ongoing issues of childhood poverty have been laid bare, and society is pushing for a better support system for our low income families. This can also be seen in the sustained need for and use of food banks with the Trussell Trust providing a network of over 1,200 food banks supported by community organisations such as schools and churches and businesses such as supermarkets to help gather the food donations from the public to be distributed to those families referred to the food banks by teachers, doctors and social workers.

Previous British governments introduced legislation (The Child Poverty Act, 2010) and targets for the eradication of child poverty with an initial target set of 2020. This was replaced, however, by the Welfare Reform and Work Act (2016) which abolished the 2010 legislation including the targets to eradicate child poverty as they were deemed unachievable. This change in policy direction also set out a clear vision that the way out of poverty is through work, and all policy and initiatives set since then have supported this direction including the 30-hour childcare support, extended schools and the ability to share parental leave after a baby is born or a child adopted.

Alongside policy being initiated to encourage working families there are clear policy pathways to reduce what is known at the *attainment gap*. The *attainment gap* refers to the education achievement levels and the disparity between children in receipt of free school meals and therefore on a low income or experiencing some other type of disadvantage and those who have their childhood in more affluent circumstances. The gap in 2020 was that disadvantaged pupils were 18.1 months behind their peers by the completion of their GCSEs with the gap increasing in primary schools for the first time in five years rather than being on a downward trajectory (EPI, 2020). The figures have yet to be released for the post-pandemic attainment gaps but are widely considered to have increased due to the levels of online learning and self-isolations that have taken place.

Social mobility and the attainment gap

The current government has a clear policy position that the route to solving the issues of poverty lies through education and *social mobility*. *Social mobility* is the way we refer to an individual or family's movement within or between the socio-economic layers in society. Intergenerational social mobility refers to the movement of a child to a social layer that differs from their parents. Although usually referred to with an emphasis on moving upwards, it can also refer to downward movement and usually relates to economic or employment status but can also relate to health status, literacy and other educational attainments such as qualification levels. The *Unlocking Talent, Fulfilling Potential* plan was released in 2017 by the Department of Education with an aim to support children and young people to reach their full potential and close the social mobility gap through education. There are four clear ambitions within the plan which include closing the 'word gap' in Early Years (literacy); closing the attainment gap in schools (GCSEs and further education qualifications); providing high quality post-16 education for all young people and supporting everyone to achieve their potential in rewarding career paths.

The government has also introduced an *Opportunity Areas* programme in 2017 with an additional £18 million of funding pledged to extend the programme into 2022. This additional funding is in addition to the original £72 million set aside for the programme and targets the entire education sector from Early Years to employment:

- Literacy
- Maths
- Attendance
- Teacher Training and recruitment
- Post-16 options and careers advice

The additional funding is intended to support social mobility in some of the most disadvantaged areas of England with a focus on:

- Attracting teachers
- Improving careers advice
- Improving educational attainment

This need for targeted support in different areas is as a result of the geographical inequalities that are experienced across the United Kingdom and aim to provide essential support in those areas where it is needed the most. These regional inequalities are explored in further depth in chapter seven when we consider the impact of environmental issues on childhoods.

Geographical inequalities

The issue of geographical inequalities is one that is becoming more and more important to address as the gap widens between affluent and disadvantaged areas with successive reports highlighting the *postcode lottery* of childhood being linked to where a child is growing and developing. Report after report demonstrates that the area in which a child grows up is becoming a clear health indicator, and child poverty reports and maps are published regularly by the End Child Poverty Coalition. These demonstrate the extent of this issue across Britain. In 2021 this report provided statistics stating that in some areas of the United Kingdom in excess of half of the children are living in poverty with the worst area at the time being local authority area of Tower Hamlets in London with 55.8% of all children living below 60% of the median national income levels (after housing costs) and the overall situation in the United Kingdom showing a poverty rate of 31% of all children, which is unacceptably high (End Childhood Poverty Coalition, 2021). While these reports highlight the issues of those families who are entitled to welfare benefit support, it cannot be ignored that the families in *working poverty* have often extreme difficulties making ends meet as the following case study explores.

CASE STUDY – FINANCIALLY STABLE?

Beverley and Sam both work at the local FE college in the cafeteria and have three children, Amy, Hannah and Carl. All three children are in primary school. Carl gets a free school meal as he is in Year 2 but Amy and Hannah take a packed lunch as they are in Year 4 and Year 6. When the first school closures happened in 2020, both Beverley and Sam were able to be at home to support the children's education as they had both been furloughed from their catering roles at the college as the majority of students were learning online and there was no need for the cafeteria to be providing food. Initially they thought being able to all be together as a family was great, and they made the most of the time together with the family taking walks and enjoying the time that was so much quieter than their usual everyday lives but their salaries were reduced by 20% as the furlough scheme only paid 80% of incomes. Prior to the pandemic they had months where money was really tight as they rent a four bedroom house in order for all the children to have their own bedroom, and they struggled to pay the gas and electric bills as well as provide the

(Continued)

children with new winter clothes each winter. Once their incomes had reduced they found that they were now struggling to provide food for everyone at home all day as Beverley and Sam had always been provided with lunch at work, and they only had to provide packed lunch for the girls as Carl was getting a free school meal. When the call to stay at home came from the government they had not realised just how long this situation would go on for so they did not adapt their budget as they thought it would only be for a few weeks. As the weeks turned into months the novelty of being at home began to wear off, and they also realised that the children sharing the one family laptop was not ideal for all three being at home, learning online. Sam's mother offered to lend them her laptop but she lives 60 miles away and was shielding as she is 74, so they were not allowed to go and visit to collect the laptop despite her offer of help. Beverley managed to get a new laptop through an online store but had to take out a credit plan to pay for it. Their overspend each month was already going on to a credit card that they could now only afford to pay the minimum amount off each month. Prior to the pandemic they only owed a furniture store for their sofas that they had bought on a four-year interest free credit arrangement but by the time the schools and colleges returned and they were both un-furloughed and returned to the workplace, they had amassed £5,000 of debt through payment plans and credit cards that they had used to keep themselves afloat during this time. The interest payments are high, and they are now struggling to meet the interest payments as well as return to their usual lifestyle that was already hard to support on their incomes before the pandemic. Beverley asks the school if there is any support they can offer but, as both parents work, their income is above the threshold for any support at the school and via the welfare benefits system. When September 2020 arrived and Amy was due to start at secondary school, the family faced the issue of buying a completely new school uniform for the new school. Again, their income was too high to meet the threshold for any help with school uniform costs so they again turned to the credit card to pay for this added expense.

This case study demonstrates how easily a family can move from being financially stable, if a little tight at times, to being in debt and unable to afford necessities like school uniform without resorting to expensive credit. The way the government measures the *poverty line* excludes many families like this from additional support that might otherwise be in place if housing costs were taken into consideration.

Third sector influence and support

Working towards an understanding of the causes of poverty and working with the issues this creates for children and families is at the heart of many charities and third sector organisations. The End Child Poverty Coalition consists of over 80 bodies across society including children's charities and welfare organisations, social justice groups, faith groups and trade unions who are united in a vision of a United Kingdom that does not have any child poverty. They do this by campaigning to raise public awareness and to promote the issue to the government. The coalition was set up in 2003 and continues to raise awareness.

The Joseph Rowntree Foundation is a social change organisation that also works to solve UK poverty. They publish an annual report on the nature and scale of poverty in the United Kingdom using a measurement system that challenges the official government measures and includes the ongoing issue of those families who are in work but still experiencing poverty. Their definition of poverty is when resources are not enough for a minimum need and includes heating the home, paying rent or mortgage and buying essentials for children. Their annual report makes a range of recommendations each year to government based on their findings.

One of the key areas of change that the combination of the third sector organisations has created is a government commitment to review the way poverty is measured in the United Kingdom. The Social Metrics Commission proposed a new measure for measuring poverty in 2018 which included taking into consideration inescapable costs such as childcare and disability as well as the more positive position of being able to access money from savings and other liquid assets. This proposal was evaluated by the Department for Work and Pensions who concluded that the proposed new approach could be used and would improve the information and evidence on poverty that was provided to the public. At the time of writing, further development and use of this has been put on hold due to the coronavirus pandemic.

Alongside the research and recommendations provided by third sector organisations is the practical support offered to families in poverty such as the food bank system previously mentioned. Other charities offer support in the form of debt advice, support for people looking for work and mental health support for all age groups including children. The vast majority of funding for these charities and support structures comes from the generosity of the general public which serves to display the underlying concerns and values of British society and an overarching desire to support those who are struggling. It also displays a recognition that government policy and support alone are not enough.

Impact of the COVID-19 pandemic

One of the key areas uncovered by the COVID-19 pandemic has been the rising awareness of the concept of *digital poverty*. With schools closing face-to-face access to all children except key workers' children and vulnerable children across two main lockdown periods in 2020 and 2021, the lack of internet access and appropriate technology to be able to undertake online learning became a glaring issue in the United Kingdom. Internet access that is taken for granted by so many of us is not the national phenomena that many believed. Many families' only internet access is via a mobile phone with a pay-as-you-go tariff that made online access to education expensive or impossible for many families. Reports appeared in the press of families with minimal internet access having to share one mobile phone between several children and parents which led to the government creating a digital access scheme for laptops and internet access dongles. During the second period of limited school access, children without adequate online provision at home were included in the group of children allowed to attend school in person. The ongoing impact of this experience of digital poverty on children's educational outcomes is yet to be fully measured but emerging data suggest that the attainment gap, as previously discussed, has increased and will take many more years to close than previously thought.

Another area of *digital divide* that has appeared is that of digital skills and the knowledge and understanding that parents needed to support their children with online school work with a suggested 22% of the UK population lacking basic digital skills prior to the COVID-19 outbreak and a clear link established between household income and internet connections with only 51% of families with a household income of between £6,000 and £10,000 having home internet access. In comparison, 99% of families with a household income in excess of £40,001 have internet access at home (Holmes and Burgess, 2021). Many schools responded to this situation by developing paper-based work packs for those children they knew were having internet access difficulties but not all schools had this knowledge or were able to support in this way.

Conclusion

The COVID-19 pandemic has created a unique and unprecedented situation not only in the United Kingdom but across the world and as we begin to emerge from the crisis there needs to be a strong anti-poverty message that threads through all policy decisions and initiatives. The Social Metrics Commission published an overview of the situation in their report *Poverty and Covid-19* (SMC, 2020) in August of 2020 to outline the impact the pandemic had created by that point. They found that the negative labour market created by lockdowns, closures, furlough, reduced hours etc. has affected those who were already experiencing *in-work* poverty to a far greater extent than others in society with many who were already on, or just below, the poverty line fallen into deeper poverty as a result of the impact of the pandemic on their employment. This chapter has explored how easily a family can move into debt through the case study and has considered how the ways poverty is measured can prevent support from being available to many families who are in need forcing them to seek credit to pay for essentials with a heavy burden of repayments and interest attached.

While the plight of children from those families who are in receipt of support through the government measurement system is still poorer compared with their more affluent peers, it cannot be just those children who we look at when we consider the role and impact of low family incomes, or poverty, on a household. Without extensive support offered by Third sector organisations such as the Trussell

Trust for food banks or the community networks providing community fridges and wardrobes, the situation for the children of the family experiencing *in work* poverty would be significantly worse.

Recommended further reading

The Joseph Rowntree Foundation Report into UK Poverty 2020/21. Available online at: https://www.jrf.org.uk/report/uk-poverty-2020-21

4 Child mental health issues – an escalating concern

CHAPTER OBJECTIVES

- To explore key issues related to child mental health
- To consider the inter-related nature of mental health issues with other health determinants
- To identify policy areas and initiatives that aim to provide support for child mental health
- To recognise the role of the third sector to provide additional support for families
- To consider the challenges that are experienced when seeking support for mental health issues and concerns

Introduction

One of the key health determinants for child health is that of mental health. Although often, but incorrectly, used as a term to suggest that there are mental health problems and issues, mental health is an aspect of health in the same way that physical health is viewed. All individuals have mental health. It can be good mental health or poor mental health. The term *mental health* should not be used as a description of poor mental health. The NHS Long Term Plan (2019) made it clear that the National Health Service provision in future would create a *parity of esteem* between physical and mental health. This means having the same care, concern, regard and funding for mental health services and mental health promotion within the United Kingdom.

Individuals experiencing good mental health are able to feel positive about themselves and their lives. They are able to enjoy spending time with others but also be comfortable alone. Good mental health leaves a person well equipped to deal with life's daily challenges. While experiencing worry and concern about problems or feeling a little low or down at times is a perfectly normal human experience, there are situations where a person's experience of these emotions escalates and they begin to significantly impact a person's life experience and potentially their longer-term outcomes. For a child, this can have serious repercussions throughout their life course.

Mental health is not static. It can change from day to day and hour to hour in response to situations across a day. These dynamic responses to daily life and experiences tend to be referred to as 'wellbeing' rather than the wider term of 'mental health' and, again, children can have good wellbeing and poor wellbeing. Identifying good wellbeing is subjective and, individuals are usually able to explain how they are feeling although small children may exhibit behavioural signs that need to be interpreted by parents and practitioners which will be discussed further in the chapter. Being aware of children's wellbeing is important in order to be aware of any escalating mental health issues that may be developing.

No Health Without Mental Health (2011)

The Government's flagship policy for supporting mental health in England and moving towards parity of esteem in the approach to physical health is the cross-government strategy document, *No Health Without Mental Health* (HM Government and Department of Health, 2011). This strategy was a new approach to mental health care in 2011 and set out clear ways that improvements in support and care would be achieved. The escalating cost of mental health care was reaching an estimated £105,000 billion at the time of its publication, and the expectation was that the cost of treatments would soar in the coming 20 years so there was a pressing need to ensure systems in place were able to be cost-effective and efficient while meeting the needs of the whole population including children. As a self-professed strategy for social justice as well as a mental health strategy, *No Health Without Mental Health* acknowledged the inequality of access and treatment for children and young people from disadvantaged family backgrounds and for black and minority ethnic (BAME) communities. Although published as policy for England, the strategy was also aimed to support the devolved nations to develop their own similar approaches. The strategy focuses on six key themes and sets out detailed approaches to support and development for each theme:

I. More people will have good mental health

II. More people with mental health problems will recover

III. More people with mental health problems will have good physical health

IV. More people will have a positive experience of care and support

V. Fewer people will suffer avoidable harm

VI. Fewer people will experience stigma and discrimination

(HM Government and Department of Health, 2011, p. 6)

The focus of the strategy is to improve outcomes for people who have mental health problems with a particular focus on employment and education and training alongside safety and crime reduction and a reduction in users of drugs and alcohol and homelessness. Although many of these seem very adult-focused, it was acknowledged that children's mental health problems are established though early life experiences and ways to support and reduce the incidence are consistently revisited in the strategy.

Mental health conditions and disorders in children

When a child's behaviours and wellbeing indicate a wider cause for concern, medical assistance should be sought because early identification of issues is paramount to providing the care and support needed to enable children to become mentally well again. The *Five Year Forward View for Mental Health* (Mental Health Taskforce, 2016) outlined the key areas of concern for mental health in England including identification, treatment and the issues with marginalisation and stigmatisation of those people experiencing mental health issues. This transformative report clearly set out the concerns with startling statistics stating that one in four adults experienced a mental health problem across their life course with half of all identifiable issues having been established by the age of 14 and three-quarters of all problems established by the age of 24. The report further identified that one in ten (10%) of all children aged 5–16 had a diagnosable mental health condition with those children from low income families having a three times higher risk of developing issues. The report also outlined the types of mental health conditions that children experience such as conduct disorders (6%), anxiety disorders (3%), attention deficit hyperactive disorder (ADHD) (2%) or depression (2%).

The concerns related to these statistics at the time were the link to poor outcomes as adults. For example, children who were diagnosed with a conduct disorder were found to be twice as likely to complete education without achieving any qualifications; were more likely to become a parent while still a teenager themselves; were four times more likely to become a drug user and twenty times more likely to spend time in prison. The report then went on to outline the lack of support available to these children and their families, citing waiting lists for appointments for psychological therapy being at 32 weeks in 2015/16 and for those children needing to have inpatient treatment in specialist facilities, the limited provision available meant that they could be provided with treatment anywhere in the country, which either meant their families had to travel long distances or not be able to visit.

Alongside the statistics for children there was concern raised that expectant mothers were also experiencing mental health problems with 20% having depression, anxiety and, in some cases, psychosis either during their pregnancy or in the child's first year with suicide being the second most common cause of maternal death. This means that the children of these families are likely to experience distressing impacts on their emotional and social development and on their cognitive development. Again, similar to the situation on treatments and support for children, the report found that specialist services for perinatal mental health was sparse with only 15% of localities having effective provision and 40% having no provision at all.

Recommendations resulting from the *Five Year Forward View for Mental Health* (Mental Health Taskforce, 2016) included having 24 hours a day, seven days a week access to mental health care in the same way that Accident and Emergencies departments provide 24 hours access to physical care. The justification for this was wide-reaching but included the aim of reducing suicides by 10% by 2020/21. Further recommendations were made relating to expectant and perinatal mothers with increased levels of support to reach an additional 30,000 women also outlined to be achieved by 2020/21. Early intervention for children and young people was expressed as a priority with a reduction in waiting times recommended, and additional access created for 70,000 more children to high-quality mental health care also outlined for implementation by 2020/21. To support these goals, the report suggested an additional £1 billion investment into mental health services was needed by the government over the subsequent five years in order to achieve the recommendations suggested in the report.

Clearly, nobody could have predicted the global pandemic situation by 2020/21 when these recommendations and goals were published, but there are key areas that should have been achieved or improved prior to COVID-19 disrupting all services and areas of life for children. Sadly this was not the case as the research focus section below explains.

WHAT DOES THE RESEARCH TELL US?

The Mental Health of Children and Young People surveys (NHS, 1999–2021), building on the 2005 report into the Mental Health of Children and Young People in Great Britain, 2004 (Green et al, 2005), which tracked changes since 1999 to mental health issues in children and young people and found that 10% of children had a diagnosable mental health disorder, further reports were commissioned and published in 2018 and 2021. These reports provide comparable data across the age ranges of 10–16-year-olds between 1999 and 2020 and data for 2–4-year-olds and 17–19-year-olds from 2017 to 2020. The series of surveys reports on the early development of the coronavirus pandemic with the 2021 publication beginning to explore the potential impact on child mental health.

The inclusion of data for the lower age group of two- to four-year-olds in the 2017 report (NHS Digital, 2018) was new and revealed that many of the mental health issues that were being experienced by the older age ranges (5–16-year-olds and 16–19-year-olds) were already established in the early years with 5.5% of the youngest age range having a diagnosable mental health condition. This rose to

16.9% of the oldest age range indicating that there may be a period where early intervention is needed to reduce the prevalence as children entered school and early adulthood to try to prevent the higher incidences of mental health issues in adults.

Pre-school children were assessed for the 2017 survey using a Development and Wellbeing Assessment tool to explore the prevalence of a range of issues. In 2017, the statistics resulting from this survey, demonstrated that one in eighteen (5.5%) of pre-school children had a diagnosed disorder at the time the data were collected. There was a gender divide in this with boys having a rate of 6.8% and girls slightly less at 4.2%. There were also demographic differences in the data collected with boys from a white ethnic background having more incidence (8.4%) than boys from a BAME background (2.9%). There was also a geographic divide with pre-school children in Northern England more commonly having issues than elsewhere in the country (9.2%). Data also demonstrated a link between low socioeconomic status of the family with pre-school children in the lowest third of income levels having more likelihood of a mental health disorder (8.9%) than those children from the higher income families (4%) which when further broken down identified that those families in receipt of welfare benefits related to low income and disability were also more likely to experience mental health disorders (10.4%). Pre-school children whose parents had a diagnosed condition were also more likely to have a diagnosable mental health disorder (14.9%).

These findings sent shockwaves through the Early Years community with many practitioners and professionals unaware of the prevalence of the issues. The conditions identified were categorised into four main types of diagnosable condition:

- *Emotional Disorders* – anxiety and depression

- *Behavioural Disorders* – repetitive and disruptive patterns of violent and aggressive behaviours

- *Hyperactivity Disorders* – for example: developmentally inappropriate episodes of inattention, impulsive behaviour and hyperactivity

- *Less Common Disorders* – for example: mental and neurodevelopmental conditions including autism and eating disorders as well as very low prevalence conditions such as psychosis, selective mutism and attachment disorders

These data then went on to contribute to government policy strategies with a Green Paper, *Transforming Children and Young People's Mental Health Provision* being published at the end of 2017 (Department of Health and Social Care and Department for Education, 2017), with the government committing to take forward all the proposals in 2018 (Department of Health and Social Care and Department for Education, 2018) and including a commitment to improving the issues in the NHS Long Term Plan (2019).

Escalating situation: extended issues from COVID-19

In 2020 there were two follow-up publications to the 2017 data (Thandi, 2020a, 2020b) where the early impact of the COVID-19 pandemic started to be explored as part of the data set, as well as comparing statistics from the 2017 report to identify any changes. The findings were quite stark with the early impact of the pandemic meaning that rates of probable mental health disorder had increased from the one in six (16%) of 5–16-year-olds in 2017 to one in nine (10.8%) by July 2020. There were no data available for pre-school children in this follow-up report as, due to the pandemic, face-to-face interviews with new participants were not achievable so the previous participants for the 2017 survey were invited to take part in an online follow-up survey. This means that the participant responses for the pre-school age range were by 2020 all of school age and now fell into the 5–16-year-old age bracket. This is also why the statistics refer to 'probable' mental health disorders as the responses were used to create an estimate to the likelihood with a scale ranging from 'unlikely' to 'possible' or 'probable' (Thandi, 2020b) based on responses to the Strengths and Difficulties Questionnaire (SDQ) used. This was the same questionnaire used for the 2017 data collection for the 5–16-year-old age range so the responses were able to be compared and contrasted to give a reliable level of evaluation. The lack of data for the two- to four-year-old population does not mean that this concern has gone away. It simply means that it has not been measurable in this round of data collection due to the impact of the COVID-19 pandemic but will be included in subsequent follow-up studies.

Supporting wellbeing in the early years

Although not able to be included in the latest iteration of the Mental Health of Children and Young People series of surveys, very young children's mental health and wellbeing is extremely important to monitor given the prevalence of diagnosable conditions that were identified in the 2017 publication. One way of approaching this is through using the Leuven Scales (Laevers, 2005) for wellbeing and engagement. These scales are part of the toolkit for monitoring wellbeing and involvement in care settings that were developed by a research team at Leuven University in Belgium, led by Dr Ferre Laevers. There are two scales – wellbeing and involvement – and each has five levels for practitioners to work with by using roughly two-minute observations of individual children to ascertain their wellbeing and their involvement in a task. While *wellbeing* is seen as being intrinsically linked to self-esteem and resilience, *involvement* measures the level of engagement in an activity to consider whether deep-level learning is taking place. The scales range through the five points from 'extremely low' to 'extremely high' with 'low', 'moderate' and 'high' in between. A link to the manual to support this toolkit, *Well-being and Involvement in Care: A process-oriented Self-evaluation Instrument for Care Settings* can be found in the further reading at the end of this chapter.

Very young children's behaviours are often the first point a practitioner will recognise that something may be unsettling the child's wellbeing. Sudden changes in behaviour such as becoming withdrawn or becoming inattentive can be indicators that something else is happening in the child's life. Although often used as key indicators to watch for from a safeguarding perspective, these changes in behaviour can also indicate the initial outward signs of low wellbeing and that a child may be in need of additional support. While awareness of the signs of autism spectrum disorders and ADHD are becoming more mainstreamed, the signs of anxiety disorders or depression in very young children are still less recognised and can be commonly missed. Common difficulties in children under five include aggression, anxiety, separation issues, difficulties settling to play or activities, sharing, self-care (such as toilet training) and tantrums or withdrawn behaviours. Early intervention is very important in supporting these children and families to avoid early stage issues developing into later childhood problems. As the research focus box demonstrates, over half of all mental health issues are established by the age of fourteen, so the Early Years is a time when early intervention could make a real difference to children's lives. Early intervention refers to the way children at risk of poor outcomes are identified and supported at an early stage to prevent problems developing or getting worse. This means that those professionals working within the Early Years sector are at a key position to note and support the behaviours of these children and to make referrals where appropriate to mitigate the impact of a potential mental health issue at an early stage.

Children and young people's mental health policy

The escalating numbers of children with mental health problems is part of a developing policy agenda, and the NHS Long Term Plan (2019) makes it clear that support for children and young people's mental health is a major objective in the coming years with clear priorities set out for the next ten years. The plan builds on the archived *Future in Mind* report (The Children and Young People's Mental Health Taskforce, 2015) that set out a five-year vision of how the mental health of children and young people could be supported. In mid-2021, a review of children and young people's mental health policy, services, funding and education was published as a House of Commons research briefing paper (Parkin and Long, 2021). The paper explored the history of children and young people's mental health policy and set out the issues as being experienced at the time of publication with acknowledgement that there had been under-investment in services for children and young people for many years which meant that the policy agendas and the desire for parity of esteem between physical and mental health had not been able to go far enough.

Issues with CAMHS/CYPMHS

Although widely known through the acronym, CAMHS, the Child and Adolescent Mental Health Service has been recently renamed to the Children and Young People's Mental Health Service (CYPMHS). The change of name is part of the reimagining of the system which is still struggling as the result of enormous under-funding pressures and a lack of resources and staffing. The resulting waiting times for children to be seen exceed the professed standards for waiting times in many cases, and many children do not even get to the waiting list as their needs are not considered pressing enough to be referred. The England Children's Commissioner published the fourth annual report into the state of children's mental health in January 2021, at the heart of the pandemic, and reported then that the government strategies outlined in the NHS Long Term Plan (2019) were inadequate for the needs of the nation. With monthly referrals to children's mental health services in England approaching 60,000 a month at the end of 2020 (up from around 28,000 a month in 2018 the rising need for services to improve has never been so clear (Lennon, The Children's Commissioner's Office, 2021). Practitioner awareness can also contribute to better outcomes for children as the following case study demonstrates.

CASE STUDY – PRACTITIONER AWARENESS OF MENTAL HEALTH

Jessie is 3 years old and has been attending her day nursery for 6 months. When she started she was bright and lively and keen to play with all the other children and get involved in most activities. She loved the role play corner and art activities. Her parents have had recent marriage difficulties, and her father moved out of the family home two weeks ago. Staff at the nursery were told that this had happened and that sometimes Dad might be collecting instead of Mum as they were trying to keep things friendly and were sharing care for Jessie and her older brother. The first signs that something was not right were just after Jessie's Mum left her having told the staff that Dad had moved out. Jessie cried and cried after Mum left, refusing to leave the doorway and holding on to the door handle. This happened on her next three sessions too, and her key person had a conversation with Mum about it. Mum then explained that the same thing had happened at the leisure centre creche when she had gone to her gym and swim group and that the creche staff had come and got her out of the pool as Jessie was so distressed. Jessie's brother has not been displaying any unusual behaviour signs so her Mum had just assumed it was an age and stage that Jessie was going through. Staff at the nursery were then able to explain to Mum that even very young children can experience anxiety during big shifts in their daily lives, especially if one parent moves out of the family home. They were able to give Mum a leaflet from the single parent charity, Gingerbread, called 'My Family's Changing' that uses a story book format to explain simply what has happened in Jessie's family. The key person was also able to explain to Mum about emotional wellbeing in very young children and what other signs to look out for, such as changes in toileting, eating habits or withdrawn behaviours. The key person also explained to Mum that the family doctor would be able to offer more advice and signpost other types of support that might be available to help Jessie as well as other members of the family if her distress did not settle over the next few sessions.

This case study demonstrates how practitioner awareness of mental health needs in young children can present and how the family can be supported through specific charities as well as seeking support from their GP if behaviours continue. The practitioner in this case study was also able to sensitively offer support to the rest of the family through an awareness that other children and Jessie's Mum may also be experiencing poor wellbeing as a result of the changes happening in their home and family life.

Time to change

One of the biggest issues surrounding mental health issues is that many people are still very lacking in knowledge of how prevalent poor mental health is and feel that it has no impact on their own lives. This can lead to stigmatisation and discrimination as their behaviour and attitudes reflect the limited understanding or misunderstanding about poor mental health. For some people, this erroneous knowledge stems from confusion with mental health disorders, such as psychosis, that have been badly portrayed in the film and media industry over previous generations before contemporary knowledge and understanding realised the inappropriateness of these portrayals. As the Health Belief Model (Glanz et al., 2002), discussed in Chapter 2, suggests, one of the key roles of health promotion is to correct people's misunderstandings or erroneous information as a way to encourage behaviour change. This can also apply to people's knowledge and understanding around mental health as it applies to others as well as to themselves or their families. As, statistically, one in four people will experience mental health issues in any one year, it is really important that health promotion takes into consideration giving people the facts to support improved attitudes and behaviours as well as to recognise developing issues within their own families or themselves.

Time to Change is a social movement that aims to change the way people think and act in relation to mental health problems so that behaviours and attitudes become supportive and understanding rather than discriminatory and creating stigmatisation. While Time to Change is not a government policy, it does have government support and is mentioned in *No Health Without Mental Health* (HM Government and Department of Health, 2011). This demonstrates the growing role of third sector organisations in health promotion. Time to Change trains and supports hundreds of mental health champions across the country to campaign and raise awareness in their communities. A wide range of employers have committed to working within the parameters of Time to Change and introduced supportive mental health strategies and policies in the workplace alongside mental health first-aid training. Thousands of schools are also part of the movement with assemblies on mental health raising awareness among school children and providing support for young mental health champions to campaign to influence their peers. Time to Change also has a strong social media presence and an online community all pushing for raised awareness and understanding to remove myths and stigma from mental health issues.

The role of the third sector and influencers

While Time to Change is a social movement, there are also a number of other very influential charities supporting children and families in particular with mental health issues and needs. Young Minds (www.youngminds.org.uk) is focused entirely on children and young people's emotional wellbeing and their mental health. The charity works towards building resilience and raising awareness of key issues including developing understanding of the internet and social media as positive tools rather than the negative connotations and assumptions often applied to these formats and mental health issues. Young Minds is keen to increase the voice of children and young people and recognise that the media has the potential to be the vehicle for their voices.

The government also has an awareness of the importance of 'voice' for children and young people and, in February 2021, appointed a Youth Mental Health Ambassador. This newly created role has a remit to advise government on the issues that really matter to children and young people and to raise the profile of mental health education and emotional wellbeing in schools. The first ambassador in this role is Dr Alex George, famous for his role in the television show *Love Island*, but also a qualified doctor in trauma care with a career in accident and emergency medicine and care. He very tragically lost his own brother to suicide and has been an active campaigner for children's mental health since. It is hoped that the combination of his clinical expertise, personal experience and 'celebrity' profile will be able to champion the government's work within the children's mental health sector and help to shape policy on improving the support available through schools, colleges and universities. Alongside this newly created role, the government has also set up a Mental Health in Education Action Group which is a coalition of a range of mental health experts, education experts and government ministers who will work with youth advocates (such as Dr Alex George) to explore and understand the impact the pandemic has had on children and young people's mental health.

Research undertaken by the many mental health organisations and charities goes a long way to developing societal understanding of the current position and needs of the country to create policy and strategy where it is needed the most. This evidence led approach feeds into government policy and is currently providing extensive knowledge and understanding of how children's emotional wellbeing and mental health has been affected by the COVID-19 pandemic. This body of knowledge on children's lived experiences can also highlight some of the positives that came out of the pandemic such as increased exercise in some cases and more family time in many cases, while exposing the wider range of inequalities that have not been conducive to supporting children and mental health issues.

Conclusion

Children's and young people's mental health is a key concern within current government policy. Funding initiatives are being rolled out as the extent of support needed to recover from the pandemic is still being recognised. The role of third sector organisations to provide up-to-date information that includes child voice of experience is essential to make sure that new policy initiative and funding are targeted where they are actually needed and not pushed in a direction that is assumed and may not be relevant. Reducing waiting times for children to be seen by mental health specialist is an essential first step towards improving the access to this sector as well as health promotion campaigns to raise awareness of how prevalent mental health issues are across our youngest age ranges. The case study in this chapter shows how times of transition for small children can be a trigger for changed behaviour linked to their mental health and the key person in this case study was knowledgeable and aware of what impact family structure changes may have on the children of the family. The key person was also deeply aware that very young children can also experience poor mental health and offered support signposting in order to avoid anything escalating further.

The implications of pre-school children having such a wide range of diagnosable issues as shown by the 2017 data (NHS Digital, 2018) suggest that mental health issues in young children may get worse before they get better as, until support is in place to recognise and understand issues in the early years, children will keep entering school with conditions that have not been acknowledged, or provided with the early intervention that is so important for coping strategies to be developed and recovery with a view to being able to lead a happy and emotionally well-balanced life in the future.

Recommended further reading

Laevers, F (2005) *Well-being and involvement in care: A process-oriented self-evaluation instrument for care settings.* Available online at: https://www.kindengezin.be/img/sics-ziko-manual.pdf

5 Effective nutrition and children's needs

CHAPTER OBJECTIVES

- Gain knowledge on the current Government policies and strategies regarding children and healthy lifestyles

- Consider the effectiveness of health promotion campaigns relating to child nutrition

- Investigate the role of the third sector to support parents to provide effective nutrition for children

- Explore the link between poor nutrition and child health and wellbeing issues

- Explore the role of healthy eating and exercise programmes to increase health and wellbeing in children

Introduction

One of the key health determinants for children is that of nutrition. From before conception, good nutrition for the mother is essential for growth and development of a foetus, and once the baby is born then good nutrition becomes a main focus to ensure the child's physical growth and development follows typical trajectories. Although physical development in relation to food and quality of food is well known, there is less emphasis on the relationship between good nutrition and wellbeing which this chapter will explore alongside the issues associated with physical growth and development.

Children's diets are seen to be important for reasons of growth and development, and much emphasis is put on children eating well but far less emphasis on developing adult knowledge and understanding of what actually constitutes a healthy diet with common confusion linking weight loss diet regimes in adults with healthy diets in general. This confusion can often create an inadequate level of nutrition in the provision of children's meals to support children's growth and development needs as well as effective support for their emotional wellbeing.

This chapter will also explore the role of government policies and initiatives to support children to achieve better nutrition and consider these in the context of issues with children who have not had optimal nutrition and healthy lifestyles to support their development. Alongside this, the chapter will consider the role of the third sector to provide knowledge and understanding to parents as well as professionals to provide healthy meals and effective nutrition for children in their care.

Malnutrition

Malnutrition is the way we describe inadequate food quality, types or amounts of food although it is often associated with countries in the developing world or economic south with pictures of babies and toddlers suffering from the effects of malnutrition prevalent in charity appeals for funding. These are diseases such as *kwashiorkor*, which is a protein deficiency, that presents as swelling on the stomach, the face, hands and feet as well as a lack of pigment in hair and skin and flaky skin patches or *marasmus*, which is due to a severe lack of protein and calorie content within the diet and typically presents as loss of body mass and not gaining weight during development. These images of children with malnutrition from the developing world tend to mask our understanding of what less extreme forms of malnutrition look like or how they may present in children in Britain. Although extreme cases with an associated diagnosis of kwashiorkor or marasmus are occasionally seen in UK hospitals, this level of severity is usually associated with child neglect or other forms of abuse. What is less visible, however, are the conditions that come with more minor deficiencies such as anaemia, which is an iron deficiency, scurvy, which is a vitamin C deficiency, or from rickets, which is a vitamin D deficiency. These conditions are on the increase in the United Kingdom with hospital admissions rising for conditions that are related to dietary deficiencies.

The National Diet and Nutrition Survey has been running since 2008 and is a rolling survey that looks at the diet, nutrient intake and nutritional status of one thousand UK residents aged over eighteen months annually, with resulting detailed reports published regularly. The most recent relates to data gathered between the ninth and eleventh year of the survey (Public Health England and Food Standards Agency, 2020) and is considered to be the only truly representative source of detailed data around types and quantities of foods and drinks consumed by the UK population. The most recent data demonstrate that while vitamin D deficiency for children under 10 is decreasing, it is rising for children between ages 11 and 18. This is important to note as dietary habits start in the early years, and so it is essential that professionals working with younger age groups are aware of the signs of nutritional deficiency and know the correct nutritional information to pass on to families and organisations providing food for children in schools and Early Years settings.

Other areas of concern demonstrated by the National Diet and Nutrition survey are that consumption of five portions of fruit and vegetables a day is still too low, despite health promotion campaigns to encourage us all to eat '5 a day' having been running since 2009, with the average consumption for children being around three portions and adults at around four portions. The consumption of 'free sugars' in children (under 18) raises concerns because of the connection to childhood obesity and those levels are decreasing but are still significantly above the recommended levels.

Healthy diets for children and how they differ from adult diets

A healthy diet should consist of the *macronutrients*: carbohydrates, proteins, fats and *micronutrients*: vitamins and minerals. The balance of these should combine to create a diet that provides the recommended intakes for a child each day. These recommended amounts are called the *dietary reference values* in the United Kingdom and are different for children than for adults. These values are a series of estimates of the amount of energy and nutrients needed by different sections of the population. The estimated values fall into three categories: *Reference Nutrient Intakes* (RNI), *Estimated Average Requirements* (EAR) and *Lower Reference Nutrient Intakes* (LRNI). RNIs relate to protein, vitamins and minerals and are the amount that most people should need for a healthy diet. EARs relates to energy needs and the LRNIs indicate the lower levels, below which the nutritional amount is unlikely to be enough for most people. For children, these Dietary Reference Values are set for the following age groups:

- 0–3 months

- 4–6 months

- 7–9 months

- 10–12 months

- 1–3 years

- 4–6 years

- 7–10 years

- 11–14 years (male)

- 11–14 years (female)

- 15–18 years (male)

- 15–18 years (female)

As can be seen from the list above, the dietary reference values are quite detailed for children across all age ranges in childhood and split between males and females around the onset of puberty, reflecting the differing needs of adolescence on children dependent on their biological sex.

Government support for healthy eating in young children

Much of the misunderstanding of what constitutes a healthy diet for a child is because a lot of the media attention to diets and food relates to the desire to lose weight from an adult body. Many of the recommended meals and foods for adults to lose weight are not appropriate for children and can create further issues. A good example of this is the use of whole milk, or full fat milk as it is sometimes called. Children aged below one year should not have cows' milk at all, and children aged one to two years should have whole milk as they need the fat and energy to help them grow and develop. Beyond the age of two, semi-skimmed milk is appropriate as long as the rest of the child's diet is balanced and healthy. Skimmed milk (1% fat or less) is not appropriate for under-fives at all as it does not contain enough calories and other important nutrients needed for the growth and development a child's body undertakes at this age range. Half a pint of milk (or 300 ml) contains around 350 mg of calcium, which is the recommended amount for children between the ages of one and three. Changing to semi-skimmed or skimmed milk is a key feature of adult weight loss regimes alongside reducing consumption of all dairy products, and often the change is made for the whole family which can leave children's diets deficient in this key source of calcium and vitamin D as well as the fats they need for growth and energy.

The government's Healthy Start Scheme supports low-income families to buy basic foods like milk and fruit. In Scotland this scheme is called Best Start Foods. This initiative provides vouchers or payments every four weeks for pregnant people and families with children under four, who are in receipt of means-tested benefits, to buy cows' milk, fruit and vegetables (fresh, frozen and tinned), infant formula milk and pulses (fresh, dried and tinned). The scheme also works with a voucher system that can be used across more than 30,000 shops in the United Kingdom to buy pregnancy vitamins, breastfeeding vitamins and vitamins for children aged 6 months to 5 years.

The government provides a system for Early Years settings to claim back the cost of one-third of a pint of milk (189 ml) per day for children attending in England and Wales, including childminding settings, under the Nursery Milk Scheme (In Scotland this is the Scottish milk and healthy snack scheme). This scheme is provided by the Department of Health and Social Care as part of the Welfare Food Regulations (1996) and is funded by the government at a cost of around £70 million a year. Older children can have milk as part of the free school meal offer for Reception, Year 1 and Year 2, and for older children milk is available as part of the free school meal offer for disadvantaged children.

The government also provides a healthy snack in school for 4–6 year olds (Reception to Year 2) in the form of the School Fruit and Vegetable Scheme. This initiative provides a piece of fruit or vegetable for every child attending a state-funded primary, infant or special school which is roughly 450 million pieces of fruit and vegetables a year to 2.3 million children. Although this scheme was put on hold during the pandemic-related lockdown to prevent food waste, it returned by July 2020 as a major contributor to healthy diets for young children.

Once children are at school, the School Food Regulations (2014) aim to provide healthy meals in school for children. These are free for all children from Reception to Year 2 and then are available to disadvantaged children beyond Year 2 for the remaining school years. The School Food Plan (Dimbleby and Vincent, 2013) set out what the best approach to the provision of school food should be and this developed into the current School Food Regulations (2014) which came into force in January 2015. The regulations are designed to support children to develop healthy eating habits and to provide the optimum amount of energy and nutrition they need for physical and cognitive development. The standards outline which foods are appropriate for school consumption and how often they should be provided. The link to explore this further is provided in the Further Reading at the end of this chapter as well as the guidance for Early Years settings.

Education for parents around healthy diets is part of the Healthy Child Programme (2009) and a key part of health promotion across the United Kingdom. This key policy area supports families from pregnancy onwards with health promotion in all areas related to nutrition such as breastfeeding and weaning as well as for healthy diets later in a child's life. Another key health promotion campaign is the Change4Life initiative, run by Public Health England, which aims to provide key messages about healthy lifestyles including nutrition and exercise. It is the flagship of the '4Life' suite of initiatives and has been running since 2009. The aim of the health promotion initiative is to give parents the knowledge and information they need to make informed choices for their families. It is used by all sections of the community including schools and the NHS to try to improve children's nutrition and their activity levels. They also collaborate with major brands and supermarkets, government departments and non-government organisations to provide informa-tion and support materials to change health outcomes and to influence behaviour choices related to health throughout the country.

Issues related to over- and under-nutrition

The government puts a lot of emphasis on provision of healthy food, education around healthy food and financial support to enable children from disadvantaged families to have access to healthy foods; however, the rolling National Diet and Nutrition Survey (2021) continually demonstrates that British children are still not achieving a basic healthy diet. Issues associated with over-nutrition include child-hood obesity rates and the longer-term implications of unhealthy diets such as developing type 2 diabetes and heart disease in later life. Less media attention is given to those issues of under nutrition that are demonstrated by the rates of children experiencing disease and ill health associated with not having had healthy balanced diets and developing issues associated with nutrient deficiencies.

Nutrient deficiencies can lead to a myriad of child development issues. A clear example is a vitamin D deficiency estimated by the NHS to affect around 16% of children in the United Kingdom. Vitamin D deficiency can lead to rickets which causes pain in the child's limbs, growth delays and deformities, delays in walking, muscle aches and weakness and associated calcium imbalances which can create muscle contractions, heart disease and seizures. Vitamin D can be absorbed from sunlight but is also present in the diet particularly in tuna, liver and beef, eggs and in fortified breakfast cereals.

Other dietary deficiencies can cause issues such as iron deficiency anaemia which can cause tiredness, pallor and poor appetite; scurvy, a condition related to vitamin C deficiency, can cause tiredness, swollen and bleeding gums and bruising easily; and constipation which is often caused by lack of fibre in the diet and low fluid intakes. All these conditions have associated low wellbeing as a result of ill health experience.

One way the government seeks to reduce the incidence of these deficiencies is through fortification of certain foods with key vitamins and minerals as part of their manufacture or processing. Fortified foods have had nutrients added to them that do not naturally occur in that food type. Foods which are commonly fortified and are a key part of children's diets are bread and breakfast cereals. Vitamins and minerals added to these items include vitamin D, vitamin B, iron and calcium as well as a full range of vitamins and minerals that are added to infant formula milk and baby foods. All white and brown bread in the United Kingdom has calcium added by law with an announcement made in September 2021 that folic acid will also become a mandatory addition to all non-wholemeal flour in the United Kingdom. Folic acid supplementation around the time of conception has been known for 30 years to prevent neural tube defects, such as spina bifida, in babies but with only 28% of pregnant people reporting that they took supplements in 2019; this planned fortification should contribute to the prevention of excessive birth defects in future.

Childhood obesity

The National Diet and Nutrition survey (2021) is a key source of information about the diet and lifestyle habits of British children and their families. This rolling survey has been collecting data since 2008 with details being included about income levels and geographical areas. The findings year on year continually support the suggestion that disadvantaged children are more likely to have poor quality diets while more affluent families are more likely to be closer to achieving the Dietary Reference Values for recommended food groups. This correlation with low income has been discussed in Chapter 3 when exploring poverty and continually arises when looking at the various differing forms of data that are collected relating to childhood obesity and effective nutrition for children.

Another key policy initiative that identifies children with rising or existing issues with their weight is the National Child Measurement Programme. This programme, which has been running since 2006, is mandatory for state-funded primary schools. The programme, run by Public Health England, provides the resources for every child to be weighed have their height measured in Reception year and again in Year 6 of primary school in order to assess the levels of children who are overweight or obese. The data gained from this annual programme are used to provide targeted support to tackle obesity by informing local planning and delivery of services to children where it is needed as well as to gather population level data about trends in growth as well as obesity. The individual data collected are also used as a way of engaging with children and families about healthy lifestyles and weight issues (NHS Digital, 2021).

Information from both of these key annual studies combines to give a clear picture on the increasing numbers of children in England who are overweight or obese. The key difference between a child being classed as overweight or obese is the measurement of their Body Mass Index (BMI). For children, this is calculated in a slightly different way to adults and takes into account the growth and develop-ment rates for these age ranges. BMI is calculated by dividing weight in kilos by the square of the child's height in metres. This is then compared with a sample of children (known as the child growth reference) from 1990 in order to take age and gender into consideration. This gives a more fluid way of identifying if a child has a weight issue rather than using the more fixed method applied to adults who have stopped growing.

One of the key aspects of the National Child Measurement Programme is the contact with parents to explain the child has measured in excess of where they may be expected to be at that age group. The idea behind this is that parents can then seek support to work with healthcare professionals to manage their child's diet and lifestyle at an early stage. Research undertaken into parental experiences of the programme, however, has found that many parents object to this programme though and find it quite offensive as their perception of weight is rooted in their own ideas of what a normal weight looks like. Many people are unaware of safe weight ranges and find their parenting skills judged when the letter comes home to suggest their child is overweight. In contrast, parents who are told that their child is a healthy weight find the programme a very positive experience, while those told their child is overweight find it a negative experience and tend to dismiss the results as lacking credibility (Gainsbury and Dowling, 2018). The programme remains the key measure for childhood weight in use across the country.

One of the key issues highlighted by the National Child Measurement Programme is that childhood obesity is still rising despite the programme being in place since 2006 and the first government policy specifically targeting this issue being intro-duced in 2016. *Childhood Obesity: A plan for action* (2016) was then updated in 2017 and the more recent policy paper for obesity, *Tackling Obesity: empowering adults and children to live healthier lives* (2020) acknowledged that obesity is the greatest long-term health challenge the country faces with statistics stating that 1 in 3 primary school children enter secondary education already overweight. This policy also notes the correlation between deprived groups and obesity with chil-dren in deprived areas twice as likely to be obese as those children living in more affluent areas. This cause for concern has strong links to poor health outcomes, including the emerging data that obese people contracting COVID-19 are more likely to be admitted to hospital and are also more likely to die from the virus compared with those people of a healthy weight. The policy introduces Public Health England's *Better Health* campaign with a new range of strategies to encourage people to look at their lifestyles and to lose weight through behaviour changes to eat better and become more active (Department of Health and Social Care, 2020).

The role of exercise

Alongside healthy diets it is very important that children take the right amount of exercise, with the UK Physical Activity Guidelines (2019) suggesting that children under 5 should be active for 3 hours a day and all other children for at least one hour a day. This creates the right energy balance when combined with a healthy diet: calories in, energy out. Being active also has an impact on a child's wellbeing with fresh air and exercise long being known to contribute to healthy childhoods with health services suggesting that physical exercise can boost self-esteem, mood, sleep quality and energy as well as reduce stress levels and the chance of developing depression, dementia and Alzheimer's disease later in life. The issue arises here with children spending longer indoors at sedentary activities such as digital gaming or watching television and other screen-based activities. Parents also need to find the time to supervise younger children in their active time which for working parents can be very difficult. In school age children, policy aims to provide this active time in school with the *School Sport and Activity Plan* (2019) aiming to develop provision so that sport and physical activity are an integral part of each child's day both during school hours and by way of after school activities. The goal of this initiative is that all school children will take part in 60 minutes of physical activity every day and contribute to the child's overall active daily time.

WHAT DOES THE RESEARCH TELL US?

Nutrition and exercise can be viewed through the lens of Bronfenbrenner's *Ecological Systems Model* (1979) previously introduced in Chapter 1 and applied in subsequent chapters, where the child is at the centre of the nested structure and the systems around the child have either a direct impact on their experience of childhood or an indirect one through impact on the adults caring for the child or through government policy and societal views and values.

The typical *microsystem* surrounding the child consists of parents and professionals in their Early Years setting or school. These are the people who provide food for the child and supervise their activity levels. The outside influences of the *macrosystem* are heavily involved though in the choices that these adults make related to the child's diet and lifestyle. While professionals have the guidance documents for food in Early Years settings and the *School Food Standards* (2015) to guide and govern what is provided for the child, parents and carers have influences from a wider variety of sources. These include their own personal history with food and exercise which is often related to their family norms and cultural backgrounds.

There is also a wide influence from media advertising suggesting that some foods are more suitable for children and are aimed at that market despite their calorie content being excessive. TV advertising by some fast food chains gives the suggestion that good parenting would include a trip to their restaurants to support them to develop good relationships with their children. This bombardment of media images that equate food with happiness and good parenting can be counterproductive to the policy campaigns and initiatives that are also trying to get their message across. While the professionals are given clear guidance on what children are allowed to consume, the counter message to parents is creating a range of issues. This is a clear example of how influential both the *macrosystem* and the *microsystem* are on a child's experience. The missing link here would be the *mesosystem* – the interactions between the professionals and the parents – where there is an opportunity to promote healthier diet and lifestyle choices by giving parents clear information and educating them about what a healthy option looks like. Sadly, as seen from parental responses to the letters received from the National Child Measurement Programme, there is much work to be done here to create a healthier weight range across the nation's children.

Influence of third sector and key celebrity figures

Children's diets have had much celebrity focus in recent years with Chef Jamie Oliver campaigning against the poor quality of school dinners in 2005 leading to the current School Food Standards (2015) that are in use today. Public influencers gain a lot of traction with media support and can serve to bridge that gap between professional knowledge and awareness and parental knowledge and understanding. This can lead to action from government departments and also from parents themselves. An example of a more recent campaign is that of the footballer Marcus Rashford during the COVID-19 pandemic. Rashford grew up in a deprived area with a reliance on school meals in his family to help feed the children. He realised that when the schools moved to online provision for most children in the March 2020 lockdown, many of those children who were reliant on a free school meal were at home with no provision being made for them. He caught media attention as a famous voice speaking out at a time when the country was already in a state of concern for the children who were not in school and public awareness was subsequently raised with the government putting an alternative system of vouchers or food parcels in place for those children. His campaigning became an ongoing mission, supported by the press, to attempt to bring in permanent change to the free school meal provision during school holidays gaining some success during the summer six-week break in 2020 and the October half-term break that same year. Since then the government has committed funding to local authorities to support the national roll out of a new scheme, The Holiday Activities and Food Programme with councils expected to offer a place to all children entitled to a free school meal. Any surplus places on these schemes should be made available to other children for a fee. These holiday clubs will offer healthy food and physical activities as part of the government commitment to half child obesity by 2030. While this appears to be a positive move to tackle some of the issues around food and exercise, the issues of who is entitled to a place on the scheme again relates to the way poverty and disadvantage is measured as previously discussed in Chapter 3. Those children of working families may find themselves excluded from a scheme that could provide excellent outcomes for them as their families may not be able to pay for the scheme, even if there are surplus spaces available to them.

Often, celebrity influencers gain traction in their campaigns by media attention but also by support from organisations within the third sector and charities. Marcus Rashford, for example, worked closely with FareShare, a charity already working to provide food to vulnerable people during the pandemic. Working together they were able to target the support where needed, lobby government to make changes and launched the Child Food Poverty taskforce, a group of more than 15 organisations that support the National Food Strategy by sharing data and case studies of British children affected by child hunger.

Jamie Oliver is still campaigning within his Food Revolution campaign with a range of strategies to make a difference to child food and health and halve child obesity by 2030. He has successfully campaigned to have a government commitment to a 9 pm watershed introduced on advertising unhealthy food both online and on TV and keeps the pressure up with his campaigns for his vision of a healthier nation.

Influencers such as Jamie Oliver and Marcus Rashford raise public awareness and bring about visible and meaningful change but also raise awareness to parents too helping change come from within the microsystem as well as the formal commitments and policy agendas in the *macrosystem*. These campaigns raise parental awareness of the role of nutrition in their child's life but do not necessarily support them to make those healthy lifestyle choices as there are greater pressures on families that can affect this type of decision as the case study below demonstrates.

CASE STUDY – FAMILY FOOD CHOICES

Jessie and Cassie have two children in primary school and both work full time in minimum wage roles. They have just enough money to pay their rent and general day-to-day expenses, but school meals are an expensive extra. The school the children attend charges £2.30 a day for a school meal. The youngest, Joe, is just about to go into Year 3 so his entitlement to the universal free school meal offer will end, and Jessie and Cassie will have to find £11.50 a week extra to add to the £11.50 a week they already pay for the eldest, Sam, to have a school dinner each day so that both boys are getting the same meal every lunchtime. This means that their family budget will need to allocate just over £90 a month for the children to have a hot meal in the middle of the day. They also cook an evening meal every day so are wondering whether it would be more cost-effective to send the boys in with

(Continued)

packed lunches instead. Cassie has worked out that a cheese sandwich, packet of crisps and a chocolate biscuit for each child would save them over £50 a month. She is unaware that this will have an impact on the healthy balance of the children's current nutrition, and potentially, their weight and wellbeing. She is also unaware that the school has strict guidelines on what can be included in a packed lunch so makes the decision to send the children in with a packed lunch when Joe moves into Year 3 next academic year.

This case study demonstrates how, for a working family, making food choices can be based around financial considerations rather than opting for the best health outcomes for the children. What may seem like small sums of money on a daily basis can mount up when looked at across a family on a monthly outgoing basis. Decisions made around where a child will access lunch from are sometimes made through necessity and focussed on family budgets but can also be through lack of awareness and understanding of what a nutritious meal looks like for a young child.

Conclusion

This chapter has demonstrated that the issues related to children's diets are complex and have strong links to other health determinants such as family income levels. Associated wellbeing that comes from a healthy diet is related to adequate consumption of the right balance of both macronutrients and micronutrients through eating a wide range of foods with an emphasis on achieving the '5 a day' of fruit and vegetables that is recommended for everyone.

Government policy has been working for a number of years towards a healthier nation with key health promotion campaigns running, such as Change4Life, with the clear message that changes to diet and exercise will provide better weight management and wellbeing for both adults and children. The stark facts remain though, that children's obesity levels are still rising and that more needs to be done to tackle this issue through a combination of health promotion campaigns and government policy initiatives.

With the cost of food predicted to rise sharply in the coming years as the wider implications of the pandemic begin to emerge across the world, the incidence of poor diets and related low wellbeing and weight gain could become an even bigger issue and threat to the wellbeing of British children than it is already. Third sector organisations are working towards finding strategies and support systems to enable families to access high-quality food at sustainable costs but government policy will need to extend to consider those families in working poverty as well as those on income-related benefits to provide the targeted support to those children who are most in need.

Recommended further reading

Example Menus for Early Years Settings in England (2017) Available online at: https://www.gov.uk/government/publications/example-menus-for-early-years-settings-in-england

School Food Standards Practical Guide (2021) Available online at: https://www.gov.uk/government/publications/school-food-standards-resources-for-schools/school-food-standards-practical-guide

6   The role of media on children's worlds

CHAPTER OBJECTIVES

- To understand the range of media use in children's lives
- To consider the role of media as a health determinant linked to emotional wellbeing
- To explore the changing use of technology in families
- To investigate the role of research to inform policy and practice
- To recognise that the impact of digital media is still emergent

Introduction

Although often considered to be a key aspect of children's lives, the role of media and the use of digital media is an important area of children's cultural worlds that cannot be overlooked or dismissed when considering health determinants. The COVID-19 pandemic has made these issues and concerns of the contemporary childhood experience more visible, with much of societal interaction having been conducted in the virtual environment of the internet. Many children have had their learning move online and not been able to attend classes for weeks at a time, while others have had a place in school throughout the pandemic as key workers' children or as vulnerable children. It is a key point to note that the government criteria for face-to-face school access was adapted before the second school closure in January 2021 to include those children without internet access or equipment, or even an appropriate place to study, as well as key workers' children and vulnerable children. Figures from the Office for National Statistics suggest that 96% of households had internet access in 2020 but, when looking at composition of households with children, this figure rose to 100% where it has remained since 2018. This does not mean, however, that all children have individual access to equipment and constant internet use, as demonstrated by the government change of criteria for school access.

Internet access within a family can range from one smartphone with pay-as-you-go access to 4G networks shared by all family members to every family member having their own devices and a fibre broadband connection as well as 4G access outside the home. The disparate access to internet and to equipment was highlighted near the start of the COVID-19 pandemic, and the digital divide was clearly identified as a major cause for concern when policy was being set for children's continued education throughout the pandemic. Digital poverty has therefore become an area of discussion across the children's sector. Concerns and issues have moved forward from the safeguarding concerns of the Byron Review in 2008 to the current concerns that children without good internet access may not have been able to get the best possible educational experience throughout the pandemic with the subsequent and ongoing impact that may have had on their educational experience and attainment.

Media and children's rights

One of the first considerations when thinking about the role of media in children's lives is what is actually meant when using the all-encompassing term 'media'. In its rawest form media means access to information or communication systems and is incorporated as Article 17 of the UN Convention on the Rights of the Child (UNCRC) (UNICEF, 1989):

> *Article 17 (access to information from the media) Every child has the right to reliable information from a variety of sources, and governments should encourage the media to provide information that children can understand. Governments must help protect children from materials that could harm them.*

This gives a key message that media has the potential to be harmful but that the right to reliable information is paramount to children achieving their rights. This type of media includes all news content (live television, online and in newspaper format) as well as other information streams such as magazines (paper-based and online) as well as educational resources. The lines tend to blur somewhat though when considering children's internet use with social media and other forms of entertainment as media use then crosses over into UNCRC Article 31:

> *Article 31 (leisure, play and culture) Every child has the right to relax, play and take part in a wide range of cultural and artistic activities.*

When the UNCRC articles were written in 1989, the current position of internet access and digital worlds were not something that had been conceived or even expected and is therefore not specifically mentioned within the UNCRC articles. However, a 'Day of Discussion' in 2014 gave the opportunity for recommendations to States around 'Digital Media and Children's Rights' (United Nations, 2014). This key day of discussion gave rise to several recommendations around access to digital media and the internet in order to achieve rights related to rest, leisure, play, recreational activities, cultural life and the arts as well as to promote access to information that would help and support those children's rights related to access to information, freedom of expression, participation and education. This put digital media firmly on the development agendas of States from 2015 onwards alongside a remit to strengthen protection for children in an online world. This need to safeguard children from the potential harm the online world can create has created divided view of children's media use and detracted from the positive aspects a digital world can create within childhood as online access and media use have become a key component of contemporary British childhoods. Concerns around content that children may access; the people with whom they may communicate; the photo and video content that they may upload; cyberbullying and harassment; and security and safety concerns related to the potential for grooming and other safeguarding issues combine to make the use of the internet by children of major concern to parents, carers and professionals alike.

Contemporary use of media

Media use in this first part of the twenty-first century has developed from access to television, books and other print formats and cinema to the current wide and varied range that includes constant access to the internet with smartphones, tablets, laptops etc. Modern childhoods before the pandemic have had virtual learning platforms for education both in the classroom to aid learning and from home to complete homework or, more recently as a result of the pandemic, to conduct many children's entire educational experience during lockdown measures. Children also have a wide range of access to games consoles and other gaming platforms such as computers and smartphones. These are also in the realm of the internet with online connectivity to most gaming being available, or conducted entirely, in an online space. The range of apps in regular use by children include social media in an array of different platforms that are accessed by children of all ages. Three out of four children aged 10–12 have been found to have a social media account (Children's Commissioner, 2018) despite a legal age limit of 13 years old on creating profiles that is related to the General Data Protection Regulations (GDPR) (2018). Within GDPR (2018) a child cannot give legal consent to share their information until they are 13 therefore are unable to give consent to have a social media profile.

> ### WHAT DOES THE RESEARCH TELL US?

Academics such as Neil Postman (1982), who researched the early days of media-rich childhoods, focused on concerns for child health and access to adult materials with a clear concern for protecting the innocence of childhood, but this view was beginning to change by the end of the twentieth century and the early years of the twenty-first century with a clear recognition developing that the advances were inevitable and that the new technologies emerging had the posi-tives potential for children to create their own spaces and become involved in production and consumption (Tapscott, 1997). This started the dual nature of attitudes towards children and digital media use – those of a positive nature and those of concern for children's health and social development. Prior to COVID-19 changing the world view of children and media concerns and issues, the main contemporary concern was for internet safety, with the Byron Review, *Safer Children in a Digital World* (Byron, 2008), outlining the key areas of recommen-dation for the government of the time to take action to protect children in the digital world as it existed in those early years of the new millennium.

Alongside this government commissioned review by Tanya Byron in the United Kingdom, theory was being developed in academic circles relating to the Millennial generation (those born between 1982 and 1996/7) who had been labelled as *Digital Natives* (Prensky, 2001). That is to say, those children and young people who had no recollection or experience of a pre-internet world and spoke the lan-guage of computers as if it were a native or first language. Those others who were acquiring digital skills as professionals or parents were labelled *digital immigrants*, reflecting the need to acquire the knowledge needed to teach those who were natives. The suggestion was that the Millennial generation and those following had different methods of absorbing knowledge due to their constant access to digital media and that, as a result, they would respond better if taught in new and innovative ways that made the best use of their preferred medium. The pandemic could be said to have created a natural experiment into children's digital skills that would never have been authorised by an academic ethics committee and has moved use beyond concerns related to safeguarding (Byron, 2008) or sexualisation and commercialisation of childhoods (Bailey, 2011) to an awareness that the use of digital media for education has been the only way forward to continue to educate all children throughout the pandemic out of necessity rather than because of quality of provision or learning styles.

Current concerns and position on children's media use

The *Digital Natives* concept was challenged as early as 2010 with Brown and Czerniewicz suggesting that labelling people as being born into something becomes problematic and is not supported by evidence from neuroscience that brains are functioning differently to previous generations. They suggest that it is access and use of technology that is what creates competency rather than generational age. This is a position that has been apparent during the COVID-19 pandemic as the division of society with internet access and equipment has become more apparent as schools and government have strived to keep chil-dren's education on track despite the stringent measures that have had to be put in place to keep the virus under control within the countries of the United Kingdom. That is not to say that the original concerns about media content have gone away. Indeed, these are more relevant now than ever before but they now have to be fitted into a new place within the contemporary discourse on children's media use. It has not been appropriate to restrict screen time when that has been the only way of learning for many children or indeed to restrict screen time for leisure use when families have not been able to access sports clubs, social clubs and activities and have been restricted to remaining at home for the vast majority of families. Children's subsequent media use and access has to be viewed within this new and emerging context especially as many children are still having sporadic online learning due to self-isolation rules as teachers and classes have positive cases identified, and children are requested to remain at home for the isolation periods.

The safeguarding concerns have remained, however, with the 2008 Bryon Review making clear recommendations for how to protect children online and the Bailey Review (2011) and subsequent Progress Report (Dept for Education, 2013) considering the sexualisation and commercialisation of childhoods. It is interesting to note that there has not been another government review in this area since 2013. There is also the connected concern due to levels of childhood obesity rising consistently that more sedentary lifestyles in modern childhoods are due to being indoors more and being entertained via media use rather than the traditional outdoor and independent play experienced by previous generations. Clearly there is a divided viewpoint on the benefits and threats of media to healthy contemporary childhoods with a range of concerns that are raised by professionals, parents and the children themselves.

WHAT DOES THE RESEARCH TELL US?

One of the key messages from research into children's media use is that asking the children themselves what their experiences are tends to give a differing message to the concerns parents and practitioners may have surrounding their digital media access and use. The *EU Kids Online Project* (2020) has been running since 2010 and has noted various changes throughout this time including exploring the risks and opportunities offered by the internet to children. The most common negative experience across the EU, found by the most recent set of data published from this study, was for children to have picked up a computer virus or spyware which echoed the findings in 2015 that children wanted education on how to avoid such things, but adults were focussed on safeguarding issues. This ongoing project found, in their 2020 data, that four out of five children receive their advice and support on internet safety from parents, teachers and friends but, if this is viewed via the suggestions that Millennial parents may not be as digitally competent as suggested by earlier *digital native* commentary, then there is a discrepancy in the provision of accurate and supportive information that children themselves have stated they need via the *EU Kids Online* project in 2015. There is also the consideration that around one-third of children have reported negative internet experiences because their parents have shared information or photographs of the child online without their consent. This gives rise to a whole set of issues of ownership of digital images by children and how to give ownership of a digital footprint and may contribute to wellbeing issues for years to come (Cazaly, 2019).

The Ofcom report into children's media use and attitudes (2020) identified that half of all 10-year-olds now own a smartphone, and use of smart speakers has overtaken use of traditional radio or other music systems. Viewing habits have changed too with online, on demand, viewing being significantly more popular than traditional live television programming, and 25% of children do not watch live television at all. Alongside this, parents have increasing concerns about content related to self-harm and with online gaming although children's critical under-standing is reported to have increased in areas related to advertising and how things are funded, such as online influencers receiving goods to promote, as an example.

Digital social lives and the role of influencers

There has also been a notable increase in social activism by children using media as their platform of choice which has been termed the 'Greta Thunberg Effect' after social activist Greta Thunberg who has demonstrated that being young is not a barrier to creating change and having a voice (Sabherwal et al., 2021). Children are also more aware of, and likely to be following, local influencers, or vloggers, within their own communities as well as the wider known national and interna-tional influencers of YouTube and similar platforms. Running parallel to these developments are the somewhat more concerning discoveries that more children are reporting having seen hateful, violent and disturbing online content. The pre-COVID-19 Ofcom report (2020) found that the delicate balance between benefits and concerns by parents is veering towards a position that the positive features of online worlds may not outweigh the risks attached. The *EU Kids Online* project also published their latest findings in 2020 with similar discoveries related to smart-phone ownership and use as well as finding that video sites in use by children are now more likely to be international, such as YouTube and Instagram, rather than national sites provided within their own countries.

The outgoing Children's Commissioner, Anne Longfield, was a keen advocate of digital safety amid a recognition that digital media plays a key role in children's worlds. The *Life in Likes* report released in 2018 enables us to see the children's subjective viewpoint on the role of internet use and social media in their worlds, particularly related to wellbeing. It was conducted with children aged 8–12 to explore the digital use of children before the age of 13 where they are able to legally have a social media profile. If this is considered alongside key reviews such as Reg Bailey's 2011 review into the sexualisation and commercialisation of childhoods, where the key finding was that for children to be children then parents had to be adults and set clear parameters of acceptability as well as role model good internet behaviours, then the findings of the *Life in Likes* report (2018) suggest that not much has changed in the intervening years despite policy mea-sures aimed to support safer internet and media use. It is quite telling that there has not been another government commissioned review into this area since 2013, and yet there are clear signs that all is not well in the world of celebrity and entertainment that provide role models for all children including those who are very young. While Disney's approach to the female lead in *Frozen* (Buck and Lee, 2013), Elsa, is to be applauded on many counts as a strong, independent and fearless character, it can also be questioned why her outfits upon coming into her magical powers needed to be quite so sexualised and adult in nature when there was a clear merchandising line planned for children of two and three years old with dressing-up outfits. This in contrast to *Snow White* in 1937 (Sharpsteen et al., 1937) who portrayed that image of femininity of the time, less a fierce leader and more a victim, who dressed demurely and sang her way through her trials and troubles waiting for a strong man to come and whisk her away from it all.

The crossover between various forms of media gives rise to consider the influential role of key platforms such as Disney and Nintendo where the associated merchandising stretches into all fields of children's worlds. This interwoven nature of children's media use is referred to as *intertextuality* and has been the subject of much academic research as well as that undertaken by marketing firms and is the subject of the following case study.

CASE STUDY – POKÉMON

Freddie is a seven-year-old boy in Year 2 of Primary School. He enjoys playing the *Pokémon* card game with other children at break and lunchtimes where they trade cards with *Pokémon* characters on. The school had some concerns about the trading nature of the games but was content that children were quietly playing at break times. Freddie enjoys watching *Pokémon* animations online and on television and has a range of *Pokémon* games that he also plays on a games console at home. His younger sister who is 3 enjoys playing *Pokémon Playhouse* with Freddie when he gets home from school, and he enjoys helping his sister learn though his favourite characters. His Dad has a game on his mobile phone that enables them to go for a walk and 'catch' *Pokémon* around their community at various locations. This gives them shared time and activity together that Freddie values. His Mum has realised that *Pokémon* is a key way to engage him in books, and so they read a *Pokémon* book at bedtime giving them a quiet, dedicated time together too. Freddie settles to sleep after his bedtime story cuddling a large Charmander plush toy (a key *Pokémon* character). On World Book Day at school, Freddie wears his Pikachu outfit (a key *Pokémon* character) and is able to share games and role play at break with his friends who also have *Pokémon* character outfits to wear.

This case study demonstrates how much one platform has the potential to enter a child's cultural world and become an inherent part of their childhood experience in a positive way that supports family time and child wellbeing but is, inherently, a commercialised aspect of Freddie's childhood.

Appropriate activities and content

Intertextuality of children's cultural worlds is a key issue when considering the role of the advertising industry and marketing products to children. Although the UK advertising industry is governed by the Advertising Standards Authority (ASA) which gives special attention to children as they are considered more vulnerable, there are still a wide range of adverts which are targeted at children. Within this, there are two key codes of practice, the *UK Code of Non-Broadcast Advertising, Sales Promotion and Direct Marketing*, known as the 'CAP Code' and *The Broadcast Committee of Advertising Practice*, known as the 'BCAP code' which promotes best practice for the advertising industry and includes issues such as what is appropriate for children to view and when. An example of this would be not placing advertising deemed to be inappropriate for children near schools or play areas. This includes anything 'sexually suggestive' which should not be placed within one hundred metres of a school and any outdoor poster advertising that is 'overtly/explicitly sexual' are now banned (Conway, 2021). There is also a level of adaptation for age-appropriate advertising which may create fear and distress, or those related to child safety, being recognised as being more of an issue for younger children than older children, and guidelines are in place to only show these types of adverts at age relevant times using sensitive scheduling and age restrictions. Age restrictions are also used for content related to betting and gaming as well as other age restricted products such as alcohol and tobacco. The most recent addition to the codes of practice are part of the government obesity strategy and includes not advertising foods that are high in fat, salt and sugar (HFSS) to children or in places where children may access them.

Age ratings are also in use for games (PEGI ratings) and films and video content (BBFC) to support parents in selecting age-appropriate content for children. The PEGI (Pan European Games Information) ratings give a rating for age appropriateness as well as indicators of content descriptors. Age restrictions in the PEGI system are PEGI 3, which is suitable for all ages; PEGI 7 which may have content that is frightening for very young children; PEGI 12 which allows non-realistic violence and language; PEGI 16 which allows more realistic violence and sexual content along with bad language and the portrayal of alcohol, illegal drugs and tobacco use and PEGI 18 which is the full adult rating for all content. These age ratings should be used alongside the content descriptors related to such things as violence, bad language, fear, gambling, sex drugs, discrimination and in-game purchases to decide whether or not they are appropriate or suitable for viewing by children (PEGI, 2017). Film content classification by the British Board of Film Classification (BBFC) may be more familiar to most with age ratings from U (suitable for all) through PG (Parental Guidance), 12 (not suitable for anyone under 12 years), 12A (persons under 12 in a cinema must be accompanied by an adult), 15 (suitable only for persons over 15 years) and 18 (suitable for adults only) with the final R18 classification reserved for works with explicit sexual or fetish content that may only be sold in licenced sex shops and licenced cinemas. Although the ratings systems have been in place for many years now, children still regularly report having watched films or played games inappropriate to their age suggesting that parents either disregard or have no knowledge or understanding of the ratings system so there is a clear area for health promotion in this field to support parents in their understanding and awareness of the role of ratings in a similar way that Reg Bailey recommended that in order for children to be children, parents had to be parents (Bailey, 2011).

The role of digital resilience

Longfield's *Life in Likes* report (2018) and the ongoing series of *Good Childhood Reports* (The Children's Society, 2006–2021) give us a clear and stark reminder that social role modelling is a key feature of children's lives and contributes to their vision of themselves in identity construction, social abilities and overall healthy attitudes to lifestyles and wellbeing. Alongside this, we have to remain aware that the current generation of parents are predominantly the Millennials who do not necessarily see concerns and issues around the commercialisation of the children's entertainment industry as they themselves grew up in similar circumstances. With 93% of children now reported to play video games (Children's Commissioner, 2019) there is a wave of concern about the amount and type of online content that children are accessing from very young ages with a key message being that we need to move beyond issues of safety to the promotion of digital resilience:

> *Children have been taught about the online world for many years now, but this is often through the narrow prism of online safety. Children also need to be equipped with digital resilience if they are to lead successful lives online.*

> (Gaming the System, Children's Commissioner, 2019, p. 29)

The body of research evidence is growing to develop our understanding and awareness of the impact of screen time on children's development with concerns raised that there is a disruptive influence on the quality and quantity of parent–child interactions, with a high use of screen-based activities, when carried out without parental support or as a shared activity. Further issues related to attachment and maternal responsiveness to children are raised alongside concerns around overstimulation and young children's abilities to filter irrelevant stimuli (Napier, 2014). With internet use and access also creating social connections, access to education, entertainment, opportunities for creativity/self-expression there is a clear divide in approaches and attitudes to children's media use and access. The government has announced its intention to give wider powers to Ofcom as an Online Harms Regulator to force social media providers to take action over harmful content that appears on their sites. Ofcom have committed, in return, to help ensure that regulation provides protection for all people online and to consider in advance of this what voluntary steps could be taken to achieve this ambition. This builds further on the Digital Economy Act (2017) that requires internet service providers to block access to extreme pornographic content to users under the age of 18 and supports development of a code of practice for providers about responses to reported online bullying and harassment. While this is a positive development, it is still veering towards child protection rather than teaching and supporting digital resilience which has been identified as a need by the Children's Commissioner for England (2019) as well as the *EU Kids Online Project* (2020).

The digital divide demonstrated by the need to continue children's education throughout the pandemic led to the UK government announcing a *Get help with technology* Programme near the start of the first UK lockdown in April 2020. Since then more than 1.3 million laptops and tablets have been distributed (at the time of writing) to students without home IT equipment as well as 4G wireless routers to support online access for these children. This combined with the change in position on which children could have a school place during the third lockdown while schools had restricted access, and many pupils were learning at home sets out the new position that internet use and access has become an integral part of British education, and families need support to be able to access this for their children. The Children's Commissioner has long been working on giving children skills they need to navigate their digital worlds with a range of reports and support materials available to parents and schools to support children to develop a healthy digital life. The *Digital 5 a Day Framework* is based on the NHS *Five Steps to Better Mental Wellbeing* and gives parents and carers clear and practical steps to achieve a healthy and balanced digital diet (Figure 6.1).

Figure 6.1   Digital 5 a Day (Children's Commissioner, 2017)

While there will be many concerns about the direction that this acknowledgement of digital worlds being a key feature of contemporary childhood, from a safeguarding and health perspective, there is also a clear line of research that was already identifying benefits to technology-enhanced learning. Savage et al. (2017) found that using technology within the Early Years Foundation Stage (EYFS) can support pro-social behaviours and improve reaction times giving cognitive benefits. They also identified benefits to motivation and to emotions as they identified positive mood states related to technology-based learning activities. Guidance and recommendations on children's screen time were published by the Chief Medical

Officer in 2019 following an extensive review of current research into children's screen use. Although no causal link was found between screen use and mental health issues this review did, however, identify that those children with mental health issues were more likely to spend time on social media and that the main areas of concern are interconnected: screen time; internet use (including social media content) and persuasive design of sites used by children. With the Children's Commissioner publishing a suggested *Statutory Duty of Care for Online Service Providers* in 2019 specifically highlights the need for providers of online content, accessed by children, to take all reasonable and proportionate care to protect them from foreseeable harm.

Social media therefore has its own influence and role in children's digital worlds and although under GDPR (2018) children under 13 are not able to give legal consent to share their data and so should not be able to have a social media profile under this age, there is a range of evidence that suggests many children as young as eight do have profiles on key social media platforms such as Snapchat, Instagram, etc. (Children's Commissioner, 2018) and are accessing the full range of material available on these sites. While the *Life in Likes* (2018) research from the Children's Commissioner demonstrated a range of use and attitudes to social media, there remains huge concern about access to some graphic content. Instagram and Facebook agreed to remove all graphic images of self-harm in early 2019 but consistent reports of such content being available break through, particularly around issues such as self-harm and anorexia, with search algorithms finding content that should have been removed and/or not promoted to users as suggested content. Twitter took a different approach and agreed that self-harm images would no longer be reported as abusive as a way to try to reduce the stigma around self-harm and suicide. The worrying large rise in teenage suicides, self-harm and mental health disorder diagnoses, however, has its own tale to tell. Although not clearly linked as a cause, it is consistently found that those children and young people with mental health issues are also heavy users of social media. While a causal link has not been established there is a strong correlation between the two that parents and practitioners should not overlook or dismiss.

Conclusion

This chapter has explored how recent technological developments appear to reinforce, and to be reinforced by, broader changes in contemporary childhoods. The lines between adult activities and children's activities are blurred as similar use and access to technology is experienced by all age ranges. This means that it is becoming harder and harder to 'protect' children from experiences and media content that parents and professionals may consider to be unsuitable or inappropriate. There is a strong reliance emerging on the role of government to instigate measures within legislation, such as the forthcoming Duty of Care Bill, as well as for providers to voluntarily take responsibility for their content. This demonstrates the bi-directional nature of the *macrosystem* and the *exosystem* in Bronfenbrenner's *Ecological Systems Model* (Bronfenbrenner, 1979) that has been explored in previous chapters to consider where government legislation and societal values create an indirect impact on an individual childhood. In the case of digital childhoods considering the role of these systems within the model enables us to consider ways to provide a safer environment for children to access and explore digital culture when we realign the emphasis of safety needs to fall on all of society. In this way children can be enabled to experience the positive aspects of digitally connected social worlds as part of their everyday contemporary British childhood experience.

The pandemic has redirected concerns around children's media and internet use to consider the related issues of digital poverty and households' abilities to access the internet on appropriate equipment for work and study. This digital poverty appears to have contributed to the widening of the attainment gap discussed in Chapter 3 when exploring the impact of the pandemic on children from low income and disadvantaged backgrounds and will be explored further in the next chapter when we explore environmental issues.

Recommended further reading

Children's Commissioner (2018) *Life in Likes*. Available online at: https://www.childrenscommissioner.gov.uk/wp-content/uploads/2018/01/Childrens-Commissioner-for-England-Life-in-Likes-3.pdf

Ofcom (2020) *Children's Media Use and Attitudes*. Available online at: https://www.ofcom.org.uk/research-and-data/media-literacy-research/childrens

7 Environmental influences

CHAPTER OBJECTIVES

- To explore how a child's environment can become a key health determinant.

- To identify what constitutes a child's environment

- To acknowledge the differences between rural and urban childhood experiences

- To consider how the environment is shaped by overlapping health determinants

- To investigate the government role in creating policy agendas to mitigate some of the wider impacts of the environment

Introduction

As previous chapters have explored, there is an inter-related nature to health determinants that means that some children have a range of combined issues affecting their childhoods. One of the key components that is raised across all health determinants is that of geographical location. Areas of deprivation have worse outcomes for children across all measures and areas of health and wellbeing. This is commonly referred to as the *postcode lottery* of childhood. The idea that where a child is growing up will also have an impact on their short-term, medium-term and long-term health outcomes. This environment influence extends across the country with income divides creating the biggest divides in experience, even across the same town or city. This really brings the 'nature vs nurture' debate into context when we consider that 'nurture' is as much about the wider influences of the macrosystem as it is about the role modelling and behaviours of the people in the child's *microsystem* (Bronfenbrenner, 1979).

In 2015, all United Nations member states adopted the 2030 Agenda for Sustainable Development Goals (UN, 2021). These seventeen goals outline the areas where work is needed in both developed and developing countries to improve health and education, reduce inequality and spur economic growth at the same time as tackling issues related to climate change and working to protect oceans and forests. This chapter will explore environmental issues related to childhood that moves us beyond the very real need to save the planet but that also explores how a child's environment can become a health determinant in its own right. The Sustainable Development Goals relating to child experience are wide, ranging from the goals for no poverty and for zero hunger which are clear health determinants, to goals for reduced inequalities and sustainable cities and communities that have a broader remit on influencing childhood through to adulthood with long-term impacts being considered.

Postcode lottery of childhood experience

The report *Poor Beginnings* (National Children's Bureau, 2015) highlighted a range of inequalities across England for children's experience of childhood that were already in place before children reached the age of five. These inequalities were sub-divided into four key measures relating to children's health and wellbeing – obesity, tooth decay, injury and school readiness – and highlighted that the area in which a child was growing up would create marked difference in their outcomes in each of these key areas of child development. This report was published in the same year that responsibility for public health was moved to Local Authorities and from there on, the Healthy Child Programme 0–5 years (2009), led by Health Visitors, became the responsibility of Local Authorities to provide this key policy area for children. This meant that there could be a targeted public health programme in place for the key areas of measurement for child health and wellbeing according to local need rather than national statistics. Deprived areas were then able to look at the key measures for the children growing up there and aim health promotion campaigns where they would make the most difference to children's outcomes.

Despite this transfer of responsibility in 2015, the most recent figures show that those children living in deprived areas are still most likely to be obese, receive hospital treatment for injury, have poor dental health and display less school readiness than those children from more affluent areas. The years of austerity that attempted to redress the issues of recession were followed closely by the COVID-19 pandemic which created further divides between childhoods. The *attainment gap* between disadvantaged children and those more fortunate children has not just stopped closing but has widened with some estimates suggesting that *learning loss* created by school closures, online learning and lockdowns has compounded the situation for all children with early figures showing a loss of 1.9 months loss in reading and 2.9 months loss in mathematics for primary-aged students (Department for Education, 2021). The *attainment gap* which had been narrowing until 2019 is now projected to increase by around 36% for disadvantaged children (Education Endowment Foundation, 2020) meaning that health promotion in deprived areas has become more important than ever in the wake of the pandemic.

Combined with geographical area and the pockets of deprivation found across Britain, children are more likely to experience disadvantage from certain sections of the community including being from black and minority ethnic (BAME) groups, living with only one parent or being from a family with three or more children. The pandemic has escalated the experiences of these children and those living in poverty as those in the lowest paid jobs are most at risk of uncertain employment during the economic repercussions of the pandemic.

Geographic access to health and education

As the *Poor Beginnings* report (National Children's Bureau, 2015) demonstrated, there are geographic differences between children's experiences of childhood when access to services is considered. This divide goes beyond the assumed North/South divide as pockets of deprivation show all over Britain. The 'Indices of Multiple Deprivation' (Ministry of Housing, Communities and Local Government, 2019) clearly shows that in England there are areas of deprivation spread right across the country with 61% of Local Authorities containing at least one of the most deprived areas in England. These indices consider deprivation across seven different measures to create an overall picture of deprivation in England. Sadly, when comparing these most recent figures to previous versions of the Indices, 88% were also in the most deprived decile in the 2015 Indices of Multiple Deprivation too, demonstrating little movement in the change of some household and family experiences. For children, Blackpool and Middlesbrough are the lowest ranked areas using these measures.

Rural vs urban childhoods

Growing up in a rural area still tends to be seen as an idyllic childhood with stereotypes abounding of playing in outdoor spaces and safe streets with few cars. The reality is that for many children growing up in rural areas there is limited access to many of the services that people living in urban spaces take for granted. This contributes to the feeling of social exclusion discussed in Chapter 3 and has a big impact on wellbeing. Government statistics identified that in 2017/18, 19% of children in rural areas were living in absolute poverty after housing costs were taken into account with this rising to 24% when considered from the perspective of relative poverty. While this is still lower than the children in urban areas (27% in absolute and 31% in relative poverty) there still remains a significantly large proportion of rural childhoods being lived within the measures of poverty, and evidence from government statistics also demonstrates that this figure has increased while urban figures have decreased (Department for Environment, Food and Rural Affairs, 2019).

One of the biggest issues with growing up in rural areas is that of access to services. For many children even a trip to the cinema is unachievable as the distances to main towns are too vast and public transport is less frequent and less affordable than in urban spaces. Poor transport links also restrict access to social activities outside school and even contact between school friends at evenings and weekends when villages are situated at such as distance from school that the children are reliant on school buses to attend their education setting. Research funded by Children in Need and published by the Centre for Mental Health found that for children aged 8–13 living in isolated areas have their mental health and wellbeing impacted by poor transport links, fewer choices locally, social isolation (especially for those children with disabilities and specific identity characteristics), poor internet access and lack of access to social activities outside school with those issues associated with working poverty being of great concern (Allwood, 2020). When this is considered alongside the knowledge that over half of all mental health issues are established by the age of 14, as discussed in Chapter 4, there are clear environmental influences that shatter the stereotypical image of the idyllic countryside or coastal childhood.

While creating an overview of issues relating to childhoods in rural areas of Scotland, it was found that low employment options and low salaries could lead to in-work poverty that was compounded by lack of access to affordable and accessible childcare, which in turn limits parental employability (Glass et al., 2020). Lack of access to high-quality Early Years settings, due to accessibility issues related to transport links, then has an ongoing impact on school readiness and the good development trajectories of the under-fives. For school-aged children, the additional cost of public transport or fuel to access out of school activities can mean that an 'affordable' sports club becomes unaffordable when the bus fare to get there and back costs more than the activity itself.

Access to support services, such as dental, medical and mental health care, can also be more restricted in rural areas. This is again due to the travel distances involved in access as much as it is due to national issues with funding and capacity. New mothers, for example, have those transport issues and associated costs attached to attending Family Centres or Hubs or even accessing Health Visitor clinics for baby health checks and vaccinations. The additional time for professionals to provide home visits also has to be factored into workloads for midwives, health visitors etc. as the distances are time-consuming for a professional caseload.

In contrast, when considering the experience of urban childhoods, much of the focus is on safe spaces to play and reduction of pollution to create open outdoor spaces designed with children in mind. The wider issues of housing become more pressing as there are reduced numbers of homes available with much higher rents or property prices which then creates higher housing costs for parents. Quality, affordable homes in urban areas replace the rural issues with transport links as being the most pressing issues to urban childhoods, with in-work poverty having an impact on a larger number of children. The Sustainable Development Goal 11 – Sustainable Cities and Communities – aims to make urban spaces inclusive, safe, resilient and sustainable (United Nations, 2021) meaning that governments must work towards urban areas being affordable and accessible to all.

One of the areas where work needs to be done to achieve sustainable urban areas is that of air pollution, with children in urban areas being exposed to 30% more pollution than adults just on the walk to school or nursery when using busy roads. Their height is a key factor here as they are closer to the exhaust fumes from vehicles on the roads. In some areas of the United Kingdom, it has been found that 12% of child asthma cases are directly relatable to pollution from vehicles and roads. Children are more susceptible to this than adults because their organs, in particular their lungs, are still developing although there is also emerging evidence of the impact of air pollution on brain development with much more research into this area being planned for future studies. There are also links being made between low birth weights in London and the amount of air pollution experienced during the pregnancy (Urban Health, 2021).

WHAT DOES THE RESEARCH TELL US?

Professor Sir Michael G. Marmot is a Professor of Epidemiology at University College London as well as Director of the UCL Institute of Health Equity and a past President of the World Medical Association. He has led research groups for over 40 years exploring health inequalities and is considered a leading expert in this field. His research has contributed to major policy shifts and development of new initiatives related to the social determinants of health and social mobility.

Following the publication of a report, *Closing the Gap in a Generation* (2008) for the Commission on Social Determinants of health set up by the World Health Organisation, Michael Marmot was asked by the Labour government of the time to lead a review into health inequalities which was published in 2010 – 'Fair Society, Healthy Lives' (Marmot et al., 2010). This review identified that there is a social gradient of health with people born into the most deprived area living, on average, seven years less than people born in the wealthier areas. This was attributed to a range of issues including housing, income, education, social isolation and disability. These are all factors that are affected by income levels of the family. The review made it clear that disadvantage starts from before birth and created six priority objectives for the government to act upon:

1. giving every child the best start in life
2. enabling all children, young people and adults to maximise their capabilities and have control over their lives
3. creating fair employment and good work for all
4. ensuring a healthy standard of living for all
5. creating and developing sustainable places and communities
6. strengthening the role and impact of ill-health prevention.

(Marmot et al., 2010)

The Institute of Health Equity published a review of progress ten years later in 2020 (Marmot et al., 2020b) and found that not only had any progress been slow but also that life expectancy had not improved at all, and many health inequalities had increased. This was the first time life expectancy had not improved since 1900 and is synonymous with a society that has not prioritised managing health inequities.

On further exploration they discovered that this is not a global position as a result of global recession and subsequent austerity measures, but that England is unique in this position with the other countries of the United Kingdom faring much better against the objectives.

At the end of 2020 Marmot published a new report that examined the COVID-19 impact and made recommendations on how to start to redress the disadvantage that had exacerbated the social and economic inequalities in society and considered the impact on physical and mental health. This report, *Build Back Fairer: The COVID-19 Marmot Review* (Marmot et al., 2020b) works with the government mantra of *build back better* and considers the social inequalities that were already in existence before the pandemic that had been identified in the preceding two reviews (Marmot et al., 2010, 2020). This report made recommendations on how to do things differently in order to create a more equal society when the pandemic has run its course. The recommendations made build upon the recommendations made in the *10 Years On* review (Marmot et al., 2020b) but explore the additional inequity of the experience of the pandemic as it relates to mortality rates linked to social gradients and ethnicity. Recommendations that particularly relate to young children include:

Long term:

- Government should prioritise reducing inequalities in Early Years development.

Medium term:

- Increase levels of spending on the Early Years, as a minimum meeting the Organisation for Economic Co-operation and Development (OECD) average, and ensure allocation of funding is proportionately higher for more deprived areas.

- Improve availability and quality of Early Years services, including Children's Centres, in all regions of England.

- Increase pay and qualification requirements for the childcare workforce

Short term:

- Allocate additional government support to Early Years settings in more deprived areas, to prevent their closure and staff redundancies.

- Improve access to availability of parenting support programmes.

- Increase funding rates for free childcare places to support providers.

(Marmot et al., 2020b)

The clear links the pandemic has demonstrated between deprived areas, crowded accommodation and health inequalities for people with a BAME background has highlighted the need to protect the physical and mental health of people through clear policy initiatives that acknowledge the inequity of experience throughout the pandemic. To put it starkly, the risk of dying of COVID-19 has been less for those people who are affluent, have been able to work from home in good quality accommodation and are white with no underlying health conditions. This is the clearest demonstration of the inequity of health experience for many generations and must be taken into consideration when planning future policy agendas aimed to reduce the inequity of health outcomes.

Childhood experience of the pandemic

Marmot also identifies that, for children, there had already been policies of austerity that had created cuts to welfare benefits, closures of children's centres and cuts in funding for Sure Start, and cuts in the funding per student within the education system prior to the start of the pandemic so England entered the pandemic in an already inadequate state for the health experience of lower income groups (Marmot et al., 2020b). The regional mortality rates from COVID-19 reflect the *postcode lottery* previously mentioned with those areas of multiple deprivation also showing as high mortality areas for COVID-19.

The experience of Early Years settings in those geographic areas has also been parallel to the Indices of Multiple Deprivation with issues related to government funding of places for three- and four-year-olds already meaning that settings were operating right at the edge of viability before the pandemic began. More settings in deprived areas have been forced to close and make staff redundant as a result of the lockdowns and containment measures, meaning that business viability of the settings just was no longer possible. This means that the children who are already living in deprived areas now have less availability of a place in a quality Early Years setting where the long-term impacts of a good quality Early Years education experience have been long known to address social inequalities and help to close the attainment gap (Marmot et al., 2020b; Sylva et al., 2003).

School age children have also had a disproportionate experience in the more deprived areas with Marmot identifying that they have experienced:

- Greater loss of learning time

- Less access to online learning and educational resources

- Less access to private tutoring and additional educational materials

- Inequalities in the exam grading systems

(Marmot et al., 2020b)

Children with special educational needs and disabilities have also experienced greater disadvantage through the experience of school and Early Years setting closures with again, a high emphasis on those children in deprived areas. Teachers in those schools are reporting that the loss of learning is far higher for all children in deprived areas compared with teachers' reports from the more affluent areas. It is thought that this is in part due to the lack of access to technology to access online learning but also due to lack of space in the home to have been able to study as previously explored in Chapter 6.

As mentioned in previous chapters, the school closures also led to free school meals being removed from 1.3 million children at the height of the first lockdown period before measures were put in place to support those families. Food insecurity in those homes also followed the geographical pattern of the indices of multiple deprivation with BAME background families 50% more likely to experience food poverty in September 2020 than white families further highlighting the *postcode lottery* of childhood experience.

Children's reported mental health issues and subjective wellbeing have also shown increasing incidence throughout the pandemic with a lack of access to appropriate services since the start of the first lockdown making gaining treatments and support far more complex and harder to access than before. The wider issues related to this difficulty in accessing treatment and support also relates to children's parents and carers with associated reports that adults more likely to experience psychological distress resulting from the pandemic is higher in young people, women and Asian ethnic origin (which has the highest increase of all ethnic groups) meaning mothers in those groups are more likely to have been experiencing issues which then affects their children's experiences.

Parents' wellbeing as a factor in child wellbeing

While children are least likely to suffer from COVID-19 as a severe illness they have all been affected by the measures imposed for the containment of the virus and the subsequent educational and social issues attached to this. Reports of increased referrals to Social Services combined with higher incidence of domestic violence and abuse within families combine to create an area of great concern for the wider environment in which children are growing and developing. More children became known to Local Authority Children's Services within the first six months of the pandemic than before and were presenting at a later stage of need than previously and were more likely to then become in need of child protection plans or proceedings (The Association of Directors of Children's Services Ltd, 2021). This marked increase has potentially come about within families that have had to cope with multiple changes and stressors in their household and lives resulting from the pandemic such as those explored in the following case study.

CASE STUDY – IMPACTING CHILDREN'S EXPERIENCES

When the first lockdown came in March 2020, Sam and Dan were both working in their nearest town and driving two cars to get to work. They have two children in Primary school – one in Reception and one in Year 2. They had always made full use

(Continued)

---

of the school's breakfast club and after school activities as a form of childcare support so only had to find additional care during school holidays when their mothers both happily took turns and came to stay. When the call came to work from home both Sam and Dan were told by their employers that their role would move to being home-based until the government changed restrictions. The school moved to online learning, and the whole family were at home together. Initially Sam and Dan were able to take turns to work with the children to supervise them and their school work but their own workloads became quite difficult to manage as a result of the children being there and needing adult support with their education. Whereas in holiday periods they had always been able to rely on their own mothers for support previously there was now a ban on entering someone else's home and both mothers were over seventy years old so were shielding on government direction. It did not take long for the frustration to set in and for both Dan and Sam to become snappy with each other and the children in what had otherwise been a very harmonious family. Frictions appeared throughout the day and culminated when Sam's employer decided that the business was no longer viable and closed leaving Sam with no employment. Although this now left Sam able to supervise the children, it also meant they were without the second income which their mortgage and bills relied upon so the arguments became more intense and louder until the neighbours were hearing them shouting on a regular basis and began to have concerns for the children with one calling Children's Services anonymously and reporting their worries about the children living within this level of conflict.

This case study demonstrates that these additional stressors on the family, combined with the loss of extended family support, have created fractures in a previously happy home and had an impact on the children's experiences. Children experiencing parental conflict has been found to be detrimental to their wellbeing and can contribute to poor outcomes in their mental health in the long term (Early Intervention Foundation, 2021).

Impact of parenting style

Good parenting is at the centre of good child wellbeing and subsequent healthy development. Sadly, parents' own wellbeing can affect their ability to parent well despite their best desires to be good parents. Stern (1985) identified that adults need to be *tuned in* to children. They need an ability to pick up on children's cues and to align their mind with the child's mind so that they can engage in a productive way that meets the child's emotional needs. When this is done, the child experiences good wellbeing and feels *understood*. With parents and carers being a key part of the child's *microsystem* (Bronfenbrenner, 1979), it is clear that their behaviours towards the child will affect the child's experience of childhood.

Parenting programmes, such as the Solihull Approach and Triple P, aim to support parents to provide the type of parenting that supports good childhoods. Parents' ability to provide the right support and attention to their children can be affected by a wide range of issues including marital or relationship breakdowns, disability within the family, domestic violence and substance misuse including alcohol. The Early Intervention Foundation (2021) have found that children who witness parental conflict can themselves develop behavioural difficulties as a way of externalising the problems and internalised issues such as low self-esteem, depression and anxiety as well as physical health problems and difficulties in social and interpersonal relationships too. The government's *Supporting Families Programme* is the latest iteration of the *Troubled Families Programme* and now has a remit to support families as recovery from the COVID-19 pandemic continues. They aim to build on the previous programme and provide support at an early stage to vulnerable children and their families that have been referred for help by Local Authority services with a hope that issues will not escalate further to the point of needing Statutory Services. The programme aims to improve a family's resilience and subsequent outcomes to prevent an issue getting worse (Ministry of Housing, Communities and Local Government, 2021). This type of support could be offered to the case study family to help them with ways to cope with the stressors being experienced as the country begins recovery from the pandemic.

Conclusion

The government has proclaimed that the recovery will create a fairer Britain and committed funding and a new raft of policy areas as we move out of the pandemic. They have begun to announce a series of initiatives to work with the various health determinants, including all those related to the child's environment, such as the *Supporting Families Programme* previously mentioned. In addition to this, they have announced a new round of funding in the 2021 budget with large allocations for the Start4Life programme and the creation of 75 Family Hubs across England. These 'Hubs' appear to be planned as a one-stop place for services to be accessed for families – much the same as the Family Centres that have lost funding and been closed for the preceding 10 years. This new wave of access for families is an effective restart of the Labour Sure Start policies of the Early Years of the new Millennium. Family Hubs have an allocated £300 million set aside for them with a focus on provision for expectant parents and for the child's first 3 years.

Issues related to the wider environment that surrounds a child in their early life are a key health determinant that cannot be excluded from our consideration of how influential the environment may be. While Bronfenbrenner (1979) identified the *microsystem* as being of key influence and the interactions in the *mesosystem* as directly influencing the child's experience of childhood, the wider *macrosystem* and the cultures and values within society are the major influence on the development of policy that directly relates to young children's lives. Policy areas are funded according to the need at the time which, right now, is focussed on recovery from the global pandemic and will remain the focus for several years to come. There will be opportunities to address historic inequalities alongside issues that have arisen from the pandemic and the development of policy and initiatives in this field is one to watch with interest in the coming years.

Recommended further reading

National Children's Bureau (2015) *Poor Beginnings: Health Inequalities among Young Children Across England.* Available online at: https://www.ncb.org.uk/sites/default/files/uploads/files/Poor%2520 Beginnings.pdf

8 The impact of physical/ genetic conditions

CHAPTER OBJECTIVES

- To consider the wide-ranging impact of disability on a family
- To explore what is meant by disability when considering childhood experience
- To acknowledge the issues related to creating an enabling society
- To recognise that the whole family is affected if any member has a disability
- To discover the inter-related nature of other health determinants to inequality created by genetic and physical health conditions

Introduction

Physical and genetic conditions have a wide impact on child health outcomes whether the condition is experienced by the child themselves or by any member of the family with whom they live. The additional care needs and cost implications have an ongoing and wide-reaching effect on every other aspect of a child's life. Despite the Equality Act (2010) outlining disability as a 'protected characteristic' this only makes discrimination on these grounds illegal. The lived experience of families with a range of disabilities moves far beyond the types of discrimination outlawed by the Act. These health inequalities are insidious to every other aspect of family life and can have a long-lasting and wide-reaching impact on child health. For this reason, physical and genetic conditions for any family member are considered as a health determinant for the child.

Disability is defined in the Equality Act (2010) as any physical or mental impairment that has substantial and long-term effects on a person's day-to-day activities. It is self-defined – that is to say that what one person considers disabling may not be considered disabling by another. Alternatively, providing adjustments can reduce the inequality to such a level that the person no longer experiences the condition as a disability. A good example of this would be poor eyesight. In our society we would no longer consider poor eyesight a disability unless it was unable to be corrected by the use of spectacles, at which point we begin to refer to it as a visual impairment. In reality, many people are heavily reliant on glasses or spectacles in order to carry out every day activities in their lives. Because the accessibility and use of glasses is so widespread, we no longer consider this a disabling condition in the way it may have been viewed 100 years ago. The impact of many conditions can be reduced by having environments that are supportive of disability, particularly those of physical disabilities, in a way that they are always there as a matter of course rather than only put into place once it is known that a person coming into the setting may need them. Good examples of this would be wider doorways and ramps on all buildings for wheelchair access and all signage also being in Braille at a pre-determined height so that those people who are visually impaired, and can read Braille, are able to find their way around buildings without support. This environmental approach to adaptations is called a *social model* of disability.

Disabling conditions in today's society are far-reaching and can range from genetic conditions experienced from birth to those that develop or become more disabling as the child grows up as well as those conditions that are acquired as a result of trauma, such as issues created by the birth itself or from accidents that leave life-changing injuries. There is also the consideration of mental health issues and conditions that have a wide-reaching effect on the entire family if any family member experiences them. All these conditions are explored together in this chapter and considered as health inequalities in their own right. The health inequalities referred to in this chapter are only examples of how conditions can affect a child and family and are not intended to be all-encompassing or exhaustive, merely illustrative of the wider issues a family may experience as a result of a family member having these conditions. The term *disability* is used as an all-encompassing term for all health and genetic conditions that have an impact on the everyday life of those families with any family member experiencing this type of condition.

WHAT DOES THE RESEARCH TELL US?

The Disabled Children's Partnership (DCP) is a coalition bringing together more than ninety organisations that campaign for improvements in health and social care for families with disabled children and young people. In 2021 they published their research report on disabled children's experiences of the COVID-19 pandemic, *Then There Was Silence: The Impact of the Pandemic on Disabled Children, Young People and their Families* (Disabled Children's Partnership and Pears Foundation, 2021). This research brought together the findings from seven earlier reports published since the start of the pandemic, alongside analysis of NHS data sets, freedom of information requests and responses from the charity sector to the pandemic.

The overwhelming theme of the research is that during times of disaster or emergency people with disabilities are disproportionately affected both during the situation and during the recovery period afterwards. This has been the case for the COVID-19 pandemic with the disruption causing children with disabilities and their families to feel *left behind, left out and locked out* (DCP, 2021, p. 4).

Disabled children's support needs are wide and varied and may impact their ability to communicate, understand and learn as well as their ability to be able to provide self-care at an age when other children are able to be independent of adult support, such as getting dressed, feeding themselves or going to the toilet. They may also need additional support to be able to have relationships with others and to socialise. The strict social distancing measures of the pandemic brought into law by the Coronavirus Act (2020) suspended the duties of Local Authorities to provide services and replaced obligations with the term *reasonable endeavours.* This has had an unprecedented effect on the multiple services used by disabled children and their families as service after service was withdrawn, or moved to an online format, leaving parents and siblings in lockdown without support services to mitigate what was already a difficult home situation but had now become beyond challenging. This situation often left parents without the ability to reduce the impact on their families, both those children with disabilities and their siblings.

Key findings of this extensive research study are that families felt that they had not been listened to across the pandemic and that the mental health and wellbeing of all the family had suffered as a result of the lack of support for their situation. Many children's reduced access to paediatric services has meant that conditions have not been able to be assessed or that conditions have got worse as many services stopped completely or were reduced and have then been very slow to return. The study also found that the charity sector responded with great flexibility and agility, not only in providing much needed support to families but also to lobby for rapid and effective policy change.

One key theme of the report is that of the stressors on relationships within the family. The recommendations made include prioritising the needs of families with disabled children in all COVID-19 recovery planning; re-assessing children to take into account regression from missed support and dealing with the backlog in assessments; putting support in place for all families to include education, health (including mental health) and provision of therapies and equipment needed as well as taking a whole family approach that includes siblings, which incorporates family activities to mitigate the isolation experienced. They also recommend identifying key investment areas for health and social care through the 2021 Comprehensive Spending Review by government.

The Disabled Children's Partnership have also recommended setting up an Early Intervention and Family Resilience Innovation Fund to provide support for the whole family throughout diagnosis including counselling, advocacy and relationship advice as a longer term solution to provide sustainable support services for families outside of the pandemic experiences and recovery (DCP, 2019).

Impact of disability on family life

The ongoing research, such as that of the Disabled Children's Partnership mentioned above, clearly expresses that a family with a child or adult member that has a disability resulting from a chronic health condition, physical impairment or genetic condition is likely to have more stressors in place that can affect good familial relationships and functioning. The added pressure of having to provide care for a family member, whether that is a child of the family or an adult in the family, has wide-reaching effects and impacts all decisions made within, and for, family life. The added time factors for providing care within the family will affect decisions about employment and who in the family is able to work as well as what hours they are able to work. This will also influence decisions about undertaking further or higher education and training. If alternative care is sought for the person with the health need, then there are cost implications attached to this, as well as consideration of the availability and quality of the care given. Decisions around the size of the family are also heavily weighted with consideration of existing family members and the available income and support for them.

Housing and living arrangements for families with a disabled member may have to take into consideration access issues within the home or proximity to health care services, thus greatly reducing the level of choice in accommodation options. Transport links are also a key area of need when medical care is needed on a regular basis. This can either involve the cost of running a car or being located within easy distance of public transport that remains accessible for the health needs. For example, London is well known for its excellent transport links, but there are only around 45% of underground stations with wheelchair access (Transport for London, 2021) and only one-fifth of railway stations nationally are accessible with step-free access to and between all platforms (Department for Work and Pensions, 2021). In contrast all black taxis in London have a wheelchair ramp available, but the cost difference between a black cab and an underground train journey is vast.

Although additional financial support may be available through the Personal Independence Payment (PIP) for adults or Disability Living Allowance (DLA) for children, there are strict eligibility criteria and the process of claiming and attending assessments has been found to be a stressor in its own right as people find it difficult to complete forms, attend assessments and explain how their needs affect everyday living. When claiming for children there is the added pressure of explaining how the child's needs may differ from another child of a similar age without the health condition. Mobility issues are not taken into account until a child reaches 3 years old for the highest rate of payment and 5 years old for the lowest rate of payment which leaves families struggling to get around with children at an age when most would be capable of walking independently for short distances.

These stressors can combine to create a high-pressure situation that has an effect on the caring adults' mental health and physical health due to the level of care some people require. There can be associated guilt or blame for both the caring adults or the family member with the health need about the impact on the family, as well as lowered self-esteem leading to a higher incidence of mental health issues. Siblings of a child with a long-term health need or disability also experience stressors that can lead to lowered wellbeing and access to normal childhood activities. In many cases siblings take on the role of carer for their brother or sister or indeed for adult family members as the whole family pulls together to meet the increased care needs within the family. All of these stressors can create a situation where there is immense pressure on family life and affect the quality of relationships within the family as well as their accommodation and family structures if the family unit becomes fractured.

Financial considerations

Although briefly touched on above, the added financial burden related to having a family member with a medical condition, health need or physical disability is wide-reaching. Research published by Scope into the additional financial burden of disability found that in 2019 the average additional cost for a disabled adult was £583 a month and for families with disabled children the additional cost was £581 a month when comparing their needs with those families without a disabled member. This figure rose to £823 a month when there were two or more disabled children in a household (John et al., 2019). Government financial support is available but, anecdotally, hard to access and some conditions have far less recognition and support than others. Children with health conditions requiring financial support have to be assessed to consider whether their needs are significantly greater than other children their age. For working families, some of the support available to families on very low incomes, such as free prescriptions for adults, is not available. All children, however, are entitled to free prescriptions until they leave tertiary (further) education settings. Disability in a family was found by the Social Metrics Measure (Social Metrics Commission, 2018) to be a factor in around half of the fourteen million families in the United Kingdom who are in poverty.

A green paper from the Department for Work and Pensions was released in 2021 for consultation – *Shaping the Future Support: the Health and Disability Green Paper* (Department for Work and Pensions, 2021). This green paper outlines the government's plan for ways to support people with disabilities and long-term health conditions alongside the National Disability Strategy (Disability Unit et al., 2021) and the Health is Everyone's Business consultation outcome (Department for Work and Pensions and Department of Health and Social Care, 2021) as a combined and holistic approach to future support with ways of limiting the opportunities experienced by people with disabilities. The National Disability Strategy is informed by the experiences of people with disabilities from a wide range of life experiences and sets out ways that people should be able to access homes, commuting to work (and school), using public transport, shopping both online and in person, accessing culture and the arts as well as outdoor activities and being able to take part in civic roles such as voting and jury service when called upon. It clearly sets out that the government vision for reducing the impact of disability is through access to work to enable people to achieve their full potential and reduce the disability employment gap (Disability Unit et al., 2021). The reality of this aim is that families with disabled members find work much harder to access – there are in excess of seven million disabled working-age people in the United Kingdom but only a little more than half of them are in work (Department for Work and

Pensions, 2021). The Disability Strategy aims to increase by one million the numbers of working-age people with disabilities and health conditions to be able to start, and remain in, employment by 2027 by improving the range of support available (Disability Unit et al., 2021).

Access to childcare for working families

A main government policy area to support families into work is that of the *30 hours childcare* offer for working parents of 3- and 4-year-olds. This *30 hours* (also known as the *extended entitlement*) is made up of the 15 hours available to all 3- and 4-year-olds, as their universal early education place, plus an additional 15 hours funded care for those parents who earn the equivalent of 16 hours on National Minimum Wage or National Living Wage a week. The funding is only provided for term time, however, so for 38 weeks a year, although parents are able to spread the hourly allocations over 50 weeks if the setting is open all year round, which gives them 22.5 hours a week funded Early Years care. The funding only covers the care or education element of the provision though and parents are asked to pay for food and other consumables such as nappies, etc. themselves. The 15 hours (or 570 hours a year) is extended to 2-year-olds where the child has a disability resulting in an Education, Health and Care Plan, or is in receipt of DLA, as well as children from the most disadvantaged backgrounds. This is partly as a support mechanism to enable parents to work but also to reduce the disadvantage the child with a disability may experience through having a health need or condition. This is part of the government initiatives designed to support closing or reducing the social mobility gap mentioned in Chapter 3.

The role of Portage

Portage is the name for the home-visiting educational service provided for families with pre-school children who have Special Educational Needs and Disabilities (SEND). Although originally developed as a home-teaching concept in Wisconsin in the United States, Portage has been a key feature of the offer for families with children with SEND since 1976 in the United Kingdom, and there are currently over 100 Portage services across England and Wales. The family is allocated a Portage Home Visitor, usually via the Local Authority, who works with the family to explore ways to help the child develop, learn, play and become a part of community in their own right. This service is designed to reduce the barriers to accessing a quality of life and education that children with SEND and their families often experience (National Portage Association, 2019). Portage Family Visitors also work with a range of Early Years settings to provide a joined up approach to the individual development plan for each child and Early Years settings, including childminders, are able to be awarded the National Portage Association Stamp of Approval if they can demonstrate that their inclusive practice aligns with the Portage Principles. The Portage Principles are key areas of practice to support children with SEND, led by

'Partnership' to offer positive and practical strategies to support the child and family to work towards small targets that combine to achieve longer term goals.

Children's experience of disability and health conditions

Around 8% of school children have a disability as defined by the Equality Act (2010). There are many more who experience health and genetic conditions requiring additional support and even more again if the age range is widened to include the Early Years before school is started. Access issues for physical needs can range from being able to reach a coat peg, to needing wheelchair access to all parts of the school without having to go on a completely different route to their peers. With over half of children with physical disabilities also having Special Educational Needs (SEN), additional support is needed to enable inclusion in all aspects of life, not just in education. A holistic approach is needed to identify and address all aspects of the child's experience with measures also taking into consideration the impact on the rest of the family – including siblings. While the government has committed to reviewing SEND practice across all levels of education, this still has a focus on education settings rather than considering all other aspect of a child and family's experience and outcomes with the National Disability Strategy focusing their aims on how to improve employment opportunities for disabled young people moving on from education into the employment sector and higher education (Department for Work and Pensions, 2021).

Hospital/peripatetic education and play therapy

Some children have physical or mental health conditions requiring long stays in hospital that also require additional support in the form of education and play. Ongoing education for these children is provided through hospital education services so that they still are able to receive an education while staying in hospital. Each Local Authority has a legal responsibility to provide ongoing education for children who have a medical condition that prevents them from attending school. This education should be full-time unless the Local Authority considers that a part-time education would be better in line with the child's needs. The National Association for Hospital Education is an organisation that supports those professionals in this field and brings together educators for children with medical needs working in hospital schools, medical pupil referral units and children and young people's mental health inpatient units. They also support peripatetic teachers who provide home visits for education for those children who are unable to attend school due to medical needs but are not inpatients in a medical setting.

Play therapy services in hospitals are a therapeutic service, rather than educational, aimed to reduce the stressful impact of staying away from home that may be experienced by a child. Being in hospital can be extremely unsettling for a child and the role of a play therapist is to attempt to reduce the fear and confusion through using play, relaxation techniques and pain management to prepare children for medical procedures or help them cope with the stress of a hospital stay. Play therapists also offer support to siblings to help them understand what is happening as well as support to parents to help them prepare the child and family for the hospital experiences.

Access to services

Quite often, when considering access to services for families that have a member with a disability or health condition, the focus is on health and education services. The stark reality for these families, however, is that access to shops, leisure centres, cinemas, theatres and all other aspects of everyday life that families without additional needs take for granted becomes far more complicated. The COVID-19 pandemic has highlighted many of the issues of online access, for example, with families just not having the technology, or the ability to use technology, to be able to access online shopping and deliveries despite being offered priority delivery slots at all major supermarkets (ONS, 2021). This meant that when asked to shield during lockdown periods, these families were unable to have reliable access to food delivery services, and many were forced out of their homes and into shops in order to provide food for the family. This situation then put those families with clinically vulnerable members at even greater risk.

Towns and high streets have access issues for people with a range of needs. While some of these needs have campaigns to address the issues, such as the Changing Places campaign that aims to provide accessible toilets for people with disabilities (Disability Unit, 2021), there still needs more support for the additional costs families face when attempting to use public transport to access all services. By increasing transport accessibility families are able to be more mobile and achieve more independence which should give them a better quality-of-life experience. With 31% of respondents to the UK Disability Survey outlining that using public spaces was difficult *often* or *all the time* (UK Disability Survey, 2021), this suggests that this is a shared experience among families with disabled members, or members with a health condition, requiring additional support. This difficulty in accessing services extends also to these leisure activities that mean that people are enabled to spend time with family and friends. Children with disabilities have been found to be three times more likely to feel lonely than children without disabilities (Sport England, 2021), and this could be a contributory factor.

Being able to have a family holiday once a year is one of the key measures of poverty used by the Social Metrics Commission. Families with a member with a health condition, or a disability, find every day access to services frustratingly complex and are therefore even less likely to achieve access to a holiday. The reality is that when they leave their more familiar home area to spend time in a place where they do not know their way around, they also do not know where the most accessible places and services are for them either. Even playgrounds provided by local authorities can fall short of inclusive provision leaving families with limited leisure options while attempting to take a holiday (Sense, 2016). Spending time as a family is very important to relationships and to good emotional wellbeing which is why it is part of the key measures of poverty. For those families with a member that has a disability, or health condition, taking a holiday can serve to reduce pressures and stressors on the whole family who undertake care needs as long as the accessibility issues are mitigated. Many children are carers to their siblings without full awareness of the role they undertake meaning that their own experience of childhood may be affected as the following case study demonstrates.

CASE STUDY – THE IMPACT ON SIBLINGS

Jasmine is 7 years old and has an older brother, Freddie, who is 9. Freddie has ADHD and presents some quite challenging behaviours both in school and in the home. Jasmine has a calming effect on Freddie, and at school she spends time with him at break times, giving him a window in the day to re-settle and calm before the next lessons. This means that Jasmine does not get a clear break time for herself to be able to play with her friends and have any down time to rebalance herself. This calming role extends to their home life where Jasmine is left to informally supervise Freddie when they are playing in the garden, watching TV or playing on their Xbox together. Their parents are very grateful that Jasmine is so good with Freddie as it gives them time to prepare meals and get things done at home, and they tell her regularly how lovely she is with her brother.

Freddie has real difficulties sleeping at night and is often awake and disturbing the whole household two or three times a night. Jasmine sometimes goes and sits on his bed and tells him long stories that she makes up on the spot to help him lie quietly and go to sleep. She has a very inventive and creative mind and Freddie loves her extended stories. This does mean, however, that Jasmine is having disturbed nights on a regular basis and sometimes struggles to stay awake in class especially after lunch when her class has story time and they all sit on the carpet to listen to the teacher read. The school is aware of Freddie's additional needs and of the role Jasmine plays in calming him down but have not considered that this role is extensive at home too and that this means that Jasmine has a caring role. Her teacher cannot understand why she gets so tired in afternoon sessions and has told her parents that she is not engaged with the classroom activities and that she needs to develop her own concentration levels. Jasmine's parents explain that she is often up at night with Freddie but the teacher just tells them that Jasmine needs plenty of sleep at her age and still does not realise that the family and Jasmine need additional support so does not refer them onwards to the SEND Coordinator to be passed to the Local Authority for a Young Carer's Needs Assessment.

This case study demonstrates how much of a role a sibling could be playing in the care of a child with a physical or genetic condition or a disability. The impact on all other aspects of the sibling's childhood experience can be wide-reaching and affect their wellbeing and their education. Awareness from all professionals working with children would help improve their experience with sensitive and thoughtful approaches to the family to raise the awareness of the role and impact of the siblings in the family.

Children as carers

One of the key issues for considering the issues of families with a member who has a health condition or genetic condition is that of the caring role of the children of the family. The case study above demonstrates the wider implications within a family of the care provided by siblings of children with health needs and disabilities. These additional responsibilities often go completely unnoticed and unsupported, with nobody seeing the wider picture of the full range of support the child is providing, or the impact that it is having on their own experience of childhood. Very often children of these families have to take on far more care duties and responsibilities than children where families do not have members with health needs. Child carers can be as young as 5 years old or even younger as the additional responsibilities can mount up quite easily. From asking a 5-year-old to help feed a sibling who cannot feed themselves to asking them to support supervision in play and care roles such as bath time. It is estimated that there are around 800,000 young carers in the United Kingdom, aged from 5 to 17 (The Children's Society, 2021), many of whom do not even realise they are carers but have the mental and physical impact of their roles on their own wellbeing nonetheless. Of more concern is that many of the Early Years or teaching staff working with these children are also unaware of the additional load these children carry in their day-to-day lives. Many young carers have to miss school or social activities in order to maintain their caring role in the family. Young carers are entitled to a *Young Carer's Needs Assessment* by the Local Authority that considers whether the child is happy to provide care and, if they are, what impact that caring role may have on their life and future outcomes. This assessment must also include recreational activities and future employment prospects and needs. Young carers are far more likely than other children to develop a mental health issue with around one-third having an identified problem prior to the pandemic. This figure is likely to have significantly increased across the course of the pandemic as early research shows that around 80% of young carers reported feeling isolated throughout the pandemic time period so far (The Children's Society, 2021).

Conclusion

This chapter has explored the wide-ranging issues experienced by families who have a family member with a physical or mental health condition or a genetic condition that requires additional support. The needs of the entire family have been considered including those of other children in the family where there is a child with a disabling condition. The complexity of family life where there are health needs by any family member are extensive and encompass all aspects of life including the broader issues of finances, access to services and education for the children of the family. This shows the clear inter-related nature of physical and genetic health conditions to the other health determinants explored in previous chapters, with a level of inequality experienced in both education and leisure activities as well as the impact on typical family life and experiences such as holidays or use of public transport.

Having a member of a family with a health need or disability can be a contributory factor to additional stressors for that family. Quite often support is targeted at the parents, or a child with a disability, but misses other children in the family whose role is often quite significant in the care of a child or parent with a disability or health need. While the case study demonstrates wider implications of recognising when support is needed, the research focus explored how the pandemic has had extended and exacerbated the situation for many families for whom health conditions are a part of their everyday life. Disability is so often viewed through the medical model of physical disability, but this chapter has demonstrated that disability can be experienced through a variety of aspects of the environment, or the infrastructure, of a community and has effects on all members of the family and not just the individual with the health need.

Recommended further reading

The Good Childhood Report (2021) *The Children's Society*. Available online at: https://www.childrens society.org.uk/information/professionals/resources/good-childhood-report-2021

Conclusion: what does the future hold?

This book has explored and discussed health determinants for children, young people and their families with the awareness that one health determinant is not experienced in isolation of the others and they all overlap and inter-relate with each other. Good health and wellbeing is a complex concept that can be overlooked in children with a focus on their physical health and development that can sometimes leave their mental health and emotional wellbeing side-lined or disregarded completely. The startling statistics that over 50% of mental health issues are established by the age of 14 (The Mental Health Taskforce, 2016) and that 5.5% of our 2–4-year-olds are already displaying diagnosable mental health conditions (NHS Digital, 2018) should be a stark warning to all who work, or intend to work, in the children's sector. These figures show that unless awareness of the issues, and the root causes of the issues, is raised, then more and more children will experience less than ideal childhoods that could set their mental health and emotional well-being on a downward trajectory, potentially affecting their outcomes as an adult.

A recurring theme of the book has been the experiences of childhood and how these can be affected by the people in the child's *microsystem* as well as the events and happenings within the *macrosystem* (Bronfenbrenner, 1979). The book has been written mid-pandemic with newly emerging data suggesting that children's lives have been disproportionately affected by the government measures put in place to attempt to contain the COVID-19 virus (Lennon, 2021) and prevent healthcare services being overwhelmed. At the time of writing, it seems like the pandemic will be being battled for a good time to come as new variants emerge and the vaccination programme in the United Kingdom races to keep up with the needs of the home nations. With this in mind, governments and professionals alike need to develop their knowledge and understanding of the issues and start to develop those policy changes and initiatives that need to happen now, and change dynamically as events unfold, to mitigate the impact of the pandemic on the next generation of adults. It cannot be disregarded that the health determinants dis-cussed in this book were already creating inequality within society for children before the pandemic, and that the experiences since March 2020 have just exac-erbated a situation that was already creating a alarming range of statistics that suggest poor experiences of childhood in Britain for many children.

While much of the emphasis in new policy is on the *catch up agenda* for school-aged children, it really cannot be ignored that our very young children have also had a huge social impact on their very formative years. Those babies born into a socially distanced world have had quieter and less social starts as parent and baby sessions were unable to run and toddler groups were closed. Even the limited family contact at the start of the pandemic when grandparents and other members of the extended family were unable to visit or be visited will have taken its toll. The lack of social contact for under-threes is still being explored, but this unprecedented situation for a society has never before been experienced so the potential impact is unknown. What we do know is that children who have traumatic childhood events, or adverse childhood experiences (ACEs), are more likely to go on to develop mental health issues in their teens or adulthood and more likely to present with unsocial behaviours within society. We also know from case studies of children who experienced severe social and physical deprivation in Romanian orphanages in the early 1990s, and were subsequently adopted by UK families (Sonuga-Barke et al., 2017), that their lack of social contact as part of extensive deprivation has had an impact on their brain development with far-reaching consequences to their adult cognitive abilities. The case studies of these Romanian children demonstrate that more than 6 months in these deprived circumstances had a correlation to poorer adult mental health outcomes. While it is not being suggested that this would happen to the babies and young children of the pandemic, it cannot be ignored that lack of social contact during a child's very early stages of development does have an impact on their attachment levels and their pro-social behaviours, with them displaying behaviours where they do not show typical wariness of strangers or depend on their usual adults as sources of security (Wismer Fries and Pollak, 2016).

Causes of concern

In Chapter 1, we explored health determinants and causes for concern, and this theme remains threaded throughout the subsequent chapters. While research is still emerging on the impact of the pandemic, we have much research evidence in place that clearly shows that the main health determinants of poverty, nutrition and mental health have wide-reaching impact in all aspects of a child's life and that of their immediate household and family. While other health determinants are explored further in the book, such as the role of media and health inequalities, these main three areas of a child's health experience do have correlation to all other aspects of a child's experience of a healthy childhood. The chapter concludes with an awareness that the part of the role of the professionals working within the children's sector encompasses health promotion in all its varied forms but suggests that all practitioners, in all professions related to children, do need training and professional development to recognise the issues related to the key health determinants and how these may present in quite a mild way but that this could mask a far greater concern and problem within the child's life.

Promoting healthy lifestyles to the right audience

In Chapter 2, the theme of health promotion was explored with the underlying hope that campaigns targeting the right audience and in the right area could create healthy and sustainable childhoods. While exploring the health promotion theories that create effective campaigns, the chapter also discussed the role of the third sector in supporting government policy development through research as well as through provision of support for children and families. This again referred us back to the *macrosystem* of Bronfenbrenner's Ecological Systems Model (1979) and suggested that if the government and third sector organisations are able to work together, then the direct positive impact on childhoods could be immense. The issues arise when funding comes to the fore, and funding streams have to be created and assigned. In times of financial complexity experienced by the country mid-pandemic, this funding assignation needs to have a clear outlook and focus towards which aspects of children's lives need most support in addition to the schools' catch up agenda for education. The lost social contact for all our children and the financial impact on many families will need to be addressed in future health promotion campaigns and, once again, a parity of esteem will be needed between a child's emotional wellbeing as well as their educational outcomes.

Financial inequalities in society

In Chapter 3, the key message was on financial inequalities and led the reader away from assuming that all financial hardship could be seen through the narrow window of who is entitled to welfare support systems and benefits. The key message was that the ways we measure poverty have to change as some of the children living in households where the parents work are the ones who experience the greatest hardships with no recourse to financial or other support from the welfare state. The focus on research considered why poverty exists within developed societies and how this can be assigned to structural systems with the ways the *poverty line* is created through government policy, and the state support is only available for those below this line. Awareness of wider issues of *working poverty* was explored through the case study and the role of third sector organisations to raise awareness through research publications. Some of these third sector organisations also provide the physical support offered through nationwide charities such as the Trussell Trust offering food banks and local community charities offering things like community fridges that provide social spaces and reduce food waste. While there will always be people at the bottom end of an income spectrum in society, this lower end does not have to create hardship for children or tough choices for parents between buying food and paying for rent or fuel. The wider society needs health promotion in place to develop their awareness and understanding of exactly how poverty can be experienced and to break the myth that poverty is related to the receipt of welfare benefits.

Children's experiences of mental health issues

In Chapter 4, the health determinant of mental health was explored with an emphasis on key issues related to child mental health as an escalating concern. The policy agenda in this field was explored alongside considering the challenges that the prevalence of mental health issues across all age groups of childhood created within society. The key message within this chapter is the knowledge that mental health issues start very young, with the statistics demonstrating that children as young as two are presenting in Early Years setting with diagnosable conditions.

Mental health awareness and training in the Early Years needs to be developed as an area of government policy with clear professional development training for Early Years practitioners in place. This would support awareness and early intervention and create the parity of esteem with physical health and cognitive abilities tracked through educational outcomes and growth and development health checks. Mental health issues are escalating, and the pandemic has likely created more cases with the latest data suggesting that a probable one in six children now have a diagnosable mental health condition (Thandi, 2020a, 2020b). This is a policy area that was already struggling to provide services and funding for all children who were referred to children and young people's mental health services even before the pandemic. A clear route to develop services alongside professional development for all persons working within the children's sector needs to be developed in order to contain this rapidly developing problem in British children.

How good nutrition can support sustainable childhoods

In Chapter 5, we explored the role of effective nutrition and considered how not meeting children's nutritional needs can lead to a range of issues, including that of childhood obesity. The links between poor emotional wellbeing and poor nutrition were discussed alongside how health promotion campaigns can support the whole family to improve and increase their exercise levels at the same time as improving their diets. Nutrition was shown throughout the chapter to be a key area of government support and policy agendas, but the support on offer falls short of that which is needed as demonstrated through key influencers, such as Marcus Rashford campaigning for food support for those children in receipt of a free school meal throughout the pandemic. This campaigning has raised the awareness that government policy initiatives were only supporting children's meals throughout term time with school holiday periods being absent from support systems for families. While the policy area appears to be changing as a result of raised public awareness through campaigns, there is still a gap at weekends and for those children in families with *working poverty*. The use of food banks by working families is increasing, and their food bank use has increased dramatically across the pandemic (Independent Food Aid Network and Feeding Britain, 2020). This overlap between nutrition and poverty as health determinants also leads into that awareness that the way poverty is measured needs to be addressed so that support can be targeted to all those children and families who need it rather than just those that fall below the poverty line and are able to receive support through policies such as Start4life and free school meals. With food prices predicted to increase sharply in the coming years of recovery from the pandemic, this is a policy area that needs addressing in order to reduce the impact on child wellbeing and families throughout Britain.

Children's digital and technological experiences

Chapter 6 moved the reader beyond the three key health determinants to consider the role of the media in healthy childhoods. This key area of children's lives has been brought to the fore by the experiences of the pandemic, not only through the extensive use of media for those children of school age but also through the extended use of media in family life for maintaining contact through video calls and for entertainment when social contacts were restricted through government measures. The chapter considers how children's media use has developed, both during and before the pandemic experiences, and explored how this could be linked to children's subjective wellbeing. While many people consider media use as a detrimental childhood experience, this chapter takes the line that media use and technology are here to stay, and restricting child use and access is not supportive in a sustainable childhood. These are skills that will be needed in their adult lives, and they should be supported to develop their use and skill in a healthy manner. The intertextuality of media use is also explored, and awareness is raised of how this can be developed in a supportive way. The chapter explores the issues of media use through the adult lens, as well as through the child lens. This includes discussion of what support children say they need to navigate digital worlds compared with the support that adults believe they need and able to offer. While the chapter has acknowledged that there are many negative impacts of media use in children's lives, it also considers that not all these are through the actions of the children themselves and that some are due to adult behaviours, such as sharing children's photos without consent. The chapter maintains throughout that technological development is inevitable and that it is becoming harder to provide protection for children against negative experiences; therefore, the policy initiatives developed in future need to be focused on raising awareness of how to manage digital lives in a healthy way as well as ways to support children to access content in a safe manner. The chapter concludes with an assertion that a culture of safety needs to be the responsibility of all of society in order that children are able to experience digital worlds in a positive and sustainable manner.

The 'postcode lottery' of childhood experience

Chapter 7 investigated the impact of where a child lives in relation to their experience of childhood. The overlaps between health determinants were discussed again in this chapter with clear awareness indicated throughout that a child's geographical experience of childhood also had a great impact on how that childhood was experienced. The *postcode lottery* of childhood was explored with reference to the areas of deprivation within Britain but also exploring the differences between a rural childhood, and the issues attached to this, and an urban childhood with its own set of concerns and health issues. The chapter introduced the sustainable development goals (United Nations, 2021) that aim to reduce inequalities and support improvements to health and education as well as work towards the environmental issues related to climate change. The chapter outlined how children's experiences of the pandemic have also been very much related to their parents' employment and the ability of Early Years settings to maintain the viability of their businesses. The issues discussed here in relation to quality Early Years education have strong links to the concerns around the widening of the attainment gap and the role of Early Years education in attempting to reduce this marked inequality in young children's lives. The increased referrals to social services were also raised as an ongoing outcome of the pandemic with a clear awareness demonstrated that parenting support through government policy initiatives needs development for all parents and not just those families already known to social services. The chapter concludes with reference back to Bronfenbrenner's Ecological Systems Model (1979) and the role of the interactions within the child's *meso-system* being influenced themselves by the values and beliefs surrounding child-hood experience in the wider societal values of the *macrosystem*. This model gives us reason to hope that the policy development will be influenced by people's own experiences as a wider proportion of the population have discovered, due to the pandemic, how important it is to maintain family relationships even when under pressures.

Family life and health inequalities

Chapter 8 considered the wide-ranging impact of overall health inequalities on family life. The key message of this chapter was that we have to look beyond the child and into the wider family and household when considering physical and genetic conditions that have a wide-ranging impact on that person's life. The chapter explored how the experience of disability and other health inequalities permeate throughout all aspects of family life and that it may not necessarily be obvious to those working with a child that the family has a member who has a disability of other health inequality. This led on to a discussion of how the other health determinants all combine and overlap within the context of families with health inequalities, exacerbating an already difficult experience of childhood for the child and family. The role of government support systems was discussed with a clear message that families' experiences of these support systems can be erratic and not necessarily provide the types of support needed. Wider issues were dis-cussed about access to services for families, with access to public transport not always as enabling as it could be and access issues experienced in all sorts of other community spaces, such as leisure services and the high street. These access issues combine to create communities that are still excluding many types of health inequality. The chapter also explores the role that many children take on as a carer to other members of their families. These roles often go unnoticed by the child themselves or even the family as their supportive role becomes normalised within that family structure. The conclusion considers how to recognise when a family needs support if a setting is only working with one member of the family and the family themselves may be unaware of the impact of the role they play in another family member's care needs. Policy agendas need strengthening to support these families alongside clear awareness within enabling policy initiatives that not all these families will be in receipt of benefits. Many families will require support in the form of an enabling infrastructure within the community that is not necessarily of a financial nature but has a great impact on a child's emotional wellbeing and experience of family life and childhood.

Recommendations for policy and practice

While The focus of this book has been on health determinants and their impact on children and young people's experience of childhood, the key theme that has emerged is that of policy initiatives and support and their potential to miss those people in the most need of their support. As a society we have a tendency to consider that only those families in receipt of welfare benefits need support and that any support offered needs to be of a financial nature or have financial implications for that family's individual budget. This book has attempted to address these issues by highlighting case studies where the families concerned have not necessarily been entitled to government support but do need additional help, either financially or through societal infrastructures that acknowledge their needs. This acknowledgement of need could then aid the development of support systems in place to recognise issues at an early stage and address them.

The role of all people working within every aspect of the children's sector is to promote good health and wellbeing for all children. Unless targeted professional development training is put in motion, the people who have the most contact with the child and the family will not know how issues can appear and therefore miss opportunities to provide information and support at the early point where it can make the most difference. Heath promotion becomes the responsibility of all people working within the children's sector, but professionals can only promote good healthy practices if they know what these are themselves.

Government policy is dynamic: it changes according to the needs of the society as highlighted by research evidence and external influences such as the global coronavirus pandemic. All policy initiatives come with a price tag, however, and while everyone agrees that a good experience of childhood should be in place for all children, the funding streams for the policies that can support this vision are not always adequate for, or indeed targeted towards, the entire section of society that needs the support. The ongoing role of the third sector to campaign, provide research evidence and develop support systems and training packages cannot be underestimated as an essential component for a country to develop sustainable and supportive childhoods and family life.

References

Allwood, L (2020) *The Space Between Us: Children's Mental Health and Wellbeing in Isolated Areas*, London: Centre for Mental Health.

Bailey, R (2011) *Letting Children be Children: Report of an Independent Review of the Commercialisation and Sexualisation of Childhood.* Available online at: https://assets.publishing.service.gov.uk/government/uploads/system/uploads/attachment_data/file/175418/Bailey_Review.pdf

Bellis, MA, Hughes, K, Leckenby, N, Perkins, C and Lowey, H (2014) National household survey of adverse childhood experiences and their relationship with resilience to health-harming behaviours in England. Available online at: https://bmcmedicine.biomedcentral.com/articles/10.1186/1741-7015-12-72

British Board of Film Classification (2021) Available online at: https://www.bbfc.co.uk/

Bronfenbrenner, U (1979) *The Ecology of Human Development: Experiments by Nature and Design*, Cambridge, MA: Harvard University Press.

Bronfenbrenner U and Ceci, SJ (1994) Nature-nurture reconceptualized in developmental perspective: A bioecological model, *Psychological Review.* 101 (4): 568–586.

Brown, C and Czerniewicz, L (2010) Debunking the 'digital native': Beyond digital apartheid, towards digital democracy, *Journal of Computer Assisted Learning* 26, 5.

Buck, C and Lee, J (2013) *Frozen.* Walt Disney Studios Motion Pictures.

Byron, T (2008) *Safer Children in a Digital World.* Available online at: https://www.iwf.org.uk/sites/default/files/inline-files/Safer%20Children%20in%20a%20Digital%20World%20report.pdf

Cazaly, H (2019) Digital media in early years settings. In **Kent, J and Moran, M** (eds), *Communication for the Early Years: A Holistic Approach.* Abingdon: Routledge.

Child Poverty Action Group (2021) Recent history of UK child poverty. Available online at: https://cpag.org.uk/recent-history-uk-child-poverty

Conway, L (2021) *Advertising to Children.* Available online at: https://commonslibrary.parliament.uk/research-briefings/cbp-8198/

Department for Digital, Culture, Media and Sport (2017) *Digital Economy Act 2017 Draft Codes of Practice and Regulations.* Available online at: https://www.gov.uk/government/publications/digital-economy-act-2017-draft-codes-of-practice-and-regulations

Department for Education (2013) *Letting Children be Children: Progress Report.* Available online at: https://assets.publishing.service.gov.uk/government/uploads/system/uploads/attachment_data/file/203333/Bailey_Review_Progress_Report.pdf

Department for Education (2017) *Unlocking Talent, Fulfilling Potential.* Available online at: https://www.gov.uk/government/publications/improving-social-mobility-through-education

Department for Education (DfE) (2018) *Working Together to Safeguard Children: A Guide to Inter-agency Working to Safeguard and Promote the Welfare of Children.* London: HM Government.

Department for Education (2021) *Understanding Progress in the 2021/21 Academic Year: Initial Findings from the Spring Term.* Available online at: https://assets.publishing.service.gov.uk/government/uploads/system/uploads/attachment_data/file/994364/Understanding_Progress_in_the_2020_21_Academic_Year_Initial_Report_3_.pdf

Department for Education and Skills (DfES) (2003) *Every Child Matters. Green Paper, Cm. 5860*. London: The Stationery Office (TSO).

Department for Environment, Food & Rural Affairs (2019) *Rural Poverty Statistics*. Available online at: https://www.gov.uk/government/statistics/rural-poverty

Department for Work and Pensions (2021) *Family Resources Survey: Financial Year 2019 to 2020*. Available online at: https://www.gov.uk/government/statistics/family-resources-survey-financial-year-2019-to-2020

Department for Work and Pensions and Department of Health and Social Care (2021) *Health Is Everyone's Business: Proposals to Reduce Ill-health Related Job Loss*. Available online at: https://www.gov.uk/government/consultations/health-is-everyones-business-proposals-to-reduce-ill-health-related-job-loss/health-is-everyones-business-proposals-to-reduce-ill-health-related-job-loss

Department of Health, 2009 *Healthy Child Programme: Pregnancy and the First Five Years of Life*, Department of Health, London.

Department of Health and Department for Children, Schools and Families, 2009, *Healthy Child Programme: From 5 to 19 Years Old*, Department of Health, London.

Department of Health and Department for Education (2017) *Transforming Children and Young People's Mental Health Provision: A Green Paper*. Available online at: https://assets.publishing.service.gov.uk/government/uploads/system/uploads/attachment_data/file/664855/Transforming_children_and_young_people_s_mental_health_provision.pdf

Department of Health and Department for Education (2018) *Government Response to the Consultation on Transforming Children and Young People's Mental Health Provision: A Green Paper and Next Steps*, Available online at: https://assets.publishing.service.gov.uk/government/uploads/system/uploads/attachment_data/file/728892/government-response-to-consultation-on-transforming-children-and-young-peoples-mental-health.pdf

Department of Health and Social Care (2017) *Childhood Obesity: A Plan for Action*. Available online at: https://www.gov.uk/government/publications/childhood-obesity-a-plan-for-action/childhood-obesity-a-plan-for-action

Department of Health and Social Care (2020) *Tackling Obesity: Empowering Adults and Children to Live Healthier Lives*. Available online at: https://www.gov.uk/government/publications/tackling-obesity-government-strategy/tackling-obesity-empowering-adults-and-children-to-live-healthier-lives

DiClemente, CC and Prochaska, JO (1998) Toward a comprehensive, transtheoretical model of change: Stages of change and addictive behaviors. In **Miller, WR and Heather, N** (eds), *Applied Clinical Psychology. Treating Addictive Behaviors*, pp3–24. New York, NY: Plenum Press. Available online at: https://doi.org/10.1007/978-1-4899-1934-2_1

Dimbleby, H and Vincent, J (2013) *The School Food Plan*. Available online at: https://assets.publishing.service.gov.uk/government/uploads/system/uploads/attachment_data/file/936238/The_School_Food_Plan.pdf

Disability Unit (2021) *UK Disability Survey Research Report, June 2021*. Available online at: https://www.gov.uk/government/publications/uk-disability-survey-research-report-june-2021

Disability Unit, Equality Hub, Department for Work and Pensions (2021) *National Disability Strategy*. Available online at: https://www.gov.uk/government/publications/national-disability-strategy

Disabled Children's Partnership (2019) Three 'Pillars' to deliver better support and care for disabled children and their families. Available online at: https://disabledchildrenspartnership.org.uk/three-pillars-to-deliver-better-support-and-care-for-disabled-children-and-their-families/

Disabled Children's Partnership and Pears Foundation (2021) *Then There Was Silence: The Impact of the Pandemic on Disabled Children, Young People and Their Families.* Available online at: https://disabled-childrenspartnership.org.uk/wp-content/uploads/2021/10/Then-There-Was-Silence-Full-Policy-Report-10-September-2021.pdf

Duffy, M and McNeish, D (2003) *What Works in Child Health.* Available online at: https://www.dmss.co.uk/pdfs/what_works_in_child_health.pdf

Early Intervention Foundation (2021) *Improving Support for Families Facing Multiple and Complex Problems.* Available online at: https://www.eif.org.uk/report/improving-support-for-families-facing-multiple-and-complex-problems

Education Endowment Foundation (2020) *Impact of School Closures on the Attainment Gap: Rapid Evidence Assessment.* Available online at: https://educationendowmentfoundation.org.uk/public/files/EEF_(2020)_-_Impact_of_School_Closures_on_the_Attainment_Gap.pdf

Education Policy Institute (2020) *Education in England: Annual Report 2020.* Available online at: https://epi.org.uk/publications-and-research/education-in-england-annual-report-2020/

End Child Poverty Coalition (2021) Available online at: http://www.endchildpoverty.org.uk/wp-content/uploads/2021/05/Local-child-poverty-indicators-report-MAY-2021_FINAL-1.pdf

Field, F (2010) *The Foundation Years: Preventing Poor Children Becoming Poor Adults. The Report of the Independent Review on Poverty and Life Chances.* London: Cabinet Office.

Gainsbury, A and Dowling, S (2018) 'A little bit offended and slightly patronised': Parents' experiences of National Child Measurement Programme feedback, *Public Health Nutrition*, 21(15), 2884-2892. doi:10.1017/S1368980018001556

General Data Protection Regulation (GDPR) (2018) Available at: https://gdpr-info.eu

Glanz, K, Rimer, BK and Lewis, FM (2002) *Health Behavior and Health Education. Theory, Research and Practice.* San Francisco, CA: Wiley & Sons.

Glass, J, Bynner, C and Chapman, C (2020) *Children and Young People and Rural Poverty and Social Exclusion: A Review of Evidence.* Glasgow: Children's Neighbourhoods Scotland.

Green, H, McGinnity, A, Meltzer, H, Ford, T and Goodman, R (2005) *Mental Health of Children and Young People in Great Britain, 2004.* Available online at: https://files.digital.nhs.uk/publicationimport/pub06xxx/pub06116/ment-heal-chil-youn-peop-gb-2004-rep1.pdf

Healthy Child Programme: Pregnancy and the First Five Years of Life. Department of Health. 2009. Available online at: https://www.gov.uk/government/publications/healthy-child-programme-pregnancy-and-the-first-5-years-of-life

HM Government and Department of Health (2011) *No Health Without Mental Health: A Cross-Government Mental Health Outcomes Strategy for People of All Ages.* Available online at: https://assets.publishing.service.gov.uk/government/uploads/system/uploads/attachment_data/file/138253/dh_124058.pdf

Hochbaum, G, Rosenstock, I and Kegels, S (1952) *Health Belief Model.* United States Public Health Service.

Holmes, H and Burgess, G (2020) *Digital Divide.* Available online at: https://www.cam.ac.uk/stories/digitaldivide

Holmes, H and Burgess, G (2021) *Digital Divide*. Available online at: https://www.cam.ac.uk/stories/digitaldivide

Hughes, K, Lowey, H, Quigg, Z and Bellis, M (2016) Relationships between adverse childhood experiences and adult mental well-being: Results from an English National Household Survey, *BMC Public Health* 16, 222.

Independent Food Aid Network and Feeding Britain (2020) *The Independent Food Aid Network and Feeding Britain Briefing October 2020, 'What Am I Supposed To Do? Is It Destitution or Prostitution'? Hunger and the Need for Food Banks Between March and September 2020*. Available online at: https://feeding-britain.org/wp-content/uploads/2020/11/IFAN-Feeding-Britain-briefing-October-2020.pdf

John, E, Thomas, G and Touchet, A (2019) *The Disability Price Tag 2019 Policy Report*. Scope. Available online at: https://www.scope.org.uk/campaigns/extra-costs/disability-price-tag/

Joseph Rowntree Foundation (2021) *UK Poverty 2020/21*. Available online at: https://www.jrf.org.uk/report/uk-poverty-2020-21

Laevers, F (2005) *Well-being and Involvement in Care: A Process-oriented Self-evaluation Instrument for Care Settings*. Available online at: https://www.kindengezin.be/img/sics-ziko-manual.pdf

Lennon, M (2021) *Children's Commissioner for England Report, The State of Children's Mental Health Services 2020/21*. Available online at: https://www.childrenscommissioner.gov.uk/wp-content/uploads/2021/01/cco-the-state-of-childrens-mental-health-services-2020-21.pdf

Lewis, O (1966) The culture of poverty, *Scientific American*, 215, 4, pp. 19–25.

Marmot, M (2004) *Status Syndrome*. London: Bloomsbury Publishing.

Marmot, M, Allen, J, Goldblatt, P, Boyce, T, McNeish, D, et al. (2010). *Fair Society, Healthy Lives – The Marmot Review: Strategic Review of Health Inequalities in England Post-2010*, London: The Marmot Review.

Marmot, M., Allen, J., Boyce, T., Goldblatt, P. and Morrison, J., (2020a), *Health Equity in England: The Marmot Review 10 Years On*, London: Institute of Health Equity.

Marmot, M., Allen, J., Goldblatt, P., Herd, E. and Morrison, J., (2020b), *Build Back Fairer, The COVID-19 Marmot Review. The Pandemic, Socioeconomic and Health Inequalities in England*, London: Institute of Health Equity.

Ministry of Housing, Communities and Local Government (2019) *English Indices of Deprivation 2019*. Available online at: https://www.gov.uk/government/statistics/english-indices-of-deprivation-2019

Ministry of Housing, Communities and Local Government (2021) *Supporting Families Programme Guidance*. Available online at: https://www.gov.uk/government/publications/supporting-families-programme-guidance-2021-to-2022

Napier, C, How use of screen media affects the emotional development of infants, *Primary Health Care* 2014 24:2, pp. 18–25.

National Children's Bureau (2015) *Poor beginnings: Health inequalities among young children across England*. Available online at: https://www.ncb.org.uk/sites/default/files/uploads/files/Poor%2520 Beginnings.pdf

National Health Service (NHS) (2019) *The NHS Long Term Plan*. Available online at: https://www.long-termplan.nhs.uk/wp-content/uploads/2019/08/nhs-long-term-plan-version-1.2.pdf

National Portage Association (2019) Available online at: Portage.org.uk

NHS Digital (2018) *Mental Health of Children and Young People in England, 2017 [PAS]*. Available online at: https://digital.nhs.uk/data-and-information/publications/statistical/mental-health-of-children-and-young-people-in-england/2017/2017#

NHS Digital (2021) *National Child Measurement Programme*. Available online at: https://digital.nhs.uk/services/national-child-measurement-programme/

NHS England (2021) *Summary of the Dental Results from the GP Patient Survey – January to March 2021*. Available online at: https://www.england.nhs.uk/statistics/wp-content/uploads/sites/2/2021/07/GP-Survey-Dental-Results-Summary-January-to-March-2021.pdf

NHS Health Scotland (2019) Adverse childhood experiences in context. Available online at: http://www.healthscotland.scot/media/2676/adverse-childhood-experiences-in-context-aug2019-english.pdf

Nintendo (2021) The Pokémon Company International. Available online at: www.Pokémon.com

Ofcom (2020) *Children's Media Use and Attitudes Report*. Available online at: https://www.ofcom.org.uk/research-and-data/media-literacy-research/childrens

Office for National Statistics (2019) *Ethnicity Pay Gaps: 2019*. Available online at: https://www.ons.gov.uk/employmentandlabourmarket/peopleinwork/earningsandworkinghours/articles/ethnicitypaygapsingreatbritain/2019

Office for National Statistics (2020a) *Gender Pay Gap in the UK: 2020*. Available online at: https://www.ons.gov.uk/employmentandlabourmarket/peopleinwork/earningsandworkinghours/bulletins/genderpaygapintheuk/2020

Office for National Statistics (2020b) *Internet Access – Households and Individuals*. Available online at: https://www.ons.gov.uk/peoplepopulationandcommunity/householdcharacteristics/homeinternetandsocialmediausage/datasets/internetaccesshouseholdsandindividualsreferencetables

Office for National Statistics (2021) *Coronavirus and the Social Impacts on Disabled People in Great Britain: February 2021*. Available online at: https://www.ons.gov.uk/peoplepopulationandcommunity/healthandsocialcare/disability/articles/coronavirusandthesocialimpactsondisabledpeopleingreatbritain/february2021

Pan European Game Information (2017) Available online at: https://pegi.info/

Parkin, E and Long, R (2021) *Children and Young People's Mental Health – Policy, CAMHS Services, Funding and Education*. Available online at: https://researchbriefings.files.parliament.uk/documents/CBP-7196/CBP-7196.pdf

Postman, N (1982) *The Disappearance of Childhood*, New York, NY, Delacorte.

Prensky, M, Digital natives, digital immigrants. In *On the Horizon*, Bradford: MCB University Press, Vol 9 No 5, October 2001.

Public Health England (2016) Health matters: Giving every child the best start in life. Available online at: https://www.gov.uk/government/publications/health-matters-giving-every-child-the-best-start-in-life

Public Health England (2020) No child left behind. Available online at: https://assets.publishing.service.gov.uk/government/uploads/system/uploads/attachment_data/file/913764/Public_health_approach_to_vulnerability_in_childhood.pdf

Public Health England (2021) Best start in life and beyond: Improving public health outcomes for children, young people and families. Available online at: https://assets.publishing.service.gov.uk/government/uploads/system/uploads/attachment_data/file/969168/Commissioning_guide_1.pdf

Public Health England and The Food Standards Agency (2020) *National Diet and Nutrition Survey: Rolling Programme Years 9 to 11 (2016/2017 to 2018/2019).* Available online at: https://assets.publishing.service. gov.uk/government/uploads/system/uploads/attachment_data/file/943114/NDNS_UK_Y9-11_report.pdf

Sabherwal, A, Ballew, MT, van der Linden, S, Gustafson, A, Goldberg, MH, Maibach, EW, Kotcher, JE, Swim, JK, Rosenthal, SA and Leiserowitz, A (2021) The Greta Thunberg Effect: Familiarity with Greta Thunberg predicts intentions to engage in climate activism in the United States, *Journal of Applied Social Psychology.* doi: 10.1111/jasp.12737

Savage M, Barnett, A and Rogers, M (2017) *Technology Enhanced Learning in the Early Years Foundation Stage.* St Albans, Critical Publishing.

Sense (2016) Making the case for play: Findings of the sense public inquiry into access to play opportunities for disabled children with multiple needs. Available online at: https://www.basw.co.uk/system/files/ resources/basw_12804-7_0.pdf

Sharpsteen, B, Morey, L, Jackson, W, Hand, D, Cottrell, W and Pearce, P (1937) *Snow White and the Seven Dwarfs.* Los Angeles, CA: RKO Radio Pictures.

Smahel, D, Machackova, H, Mascheroni, G, Dedkova, L, Staksrud, E, Ólafsson, K, Livingstone, S and Hasebrink, U (2020) *EU Kids Online 2020 Survey Results from 19 Countries.* Available online at: https:// www.lse.ac.uk/media-and-communications/assets/documents/research/eu-kids-online/reports/EU-Kids-Online-2020-10Feb2020.pdf

Social Metrics Commission (2018) *A New Measure of Poverty for the UK.* Available online at: https:// socialmetricscommission.org.uk/wp-content/uploads/2019/07/SMC_measuring-poverty-201809_summary-report.pdf

Social Metrics Commission (2020) *Poverty and Covid-19.* Available online at: https://socialmetrics-commission.org.uk/wp-content/uploads/2020/08/SMC-Poverty-and-Covid-Report.pdf

Sonuga-Barke, E, Kennedy, M, Kumsta, R, Knights, N, Golm, D, Rutter, M, Maughan, B, Schlotz, W and Kreppner, J (2017) Child-to-adult neurodevelopmental and mental health trajectories after early life deprivation: The young adult follow-up of the longitudinal English and Romanian Adoptees study *The Lancet,* 389, 10078, 1539-1548.

Sport England (2021) *Active Lives Children and Young People Survey, Academic Year 2019/20.* Available online at: https://sportengland-production-files.s3.eu-west-2.amazonaws.com/s3fs-public/2021-01/Active% 20Lives%20Children%20Survey%20Academic%20Year%2019-20%20report.pdf?VersionId=4Ti_0V0m9s Yy5HwQjSiJN7Xj.VInpjV6

Stern, D (1985) *The Interpersonal World of the Infant: A View from Psychoanalysis Developmental Psy-chology.* Available online at: https://link.springer.com/article/10.1007/BF03174535

Sylva, K, Melhuish, E, Sammons, P, Siraj, I and Taggart, B (2003) *The Effective Provision of Pre-School Education (EPPE) Project Technical Paper 12: The Final Report - Effective Pre-School Education.* Available online at: https://www.researchgate.net/publication/320194757_The_Effective_Provision_of_Pre-School_ Education_EPPE_Project_Technical_Paper_12_The_Final_Report_-_Effective_Pre-School_Education

Tapscott, N (1997) *Growing Up Digital.* Available online at: http://www.growingupdigital.com/

Thandi, S (2020a) *Mental Health of Children and Young People in England, 2020: Wave 1 Follow Up to the 2017 Survey.* Available online at: https://digital.nhs.uk/data-and-information/publications/statistical/mental-health-of-children-and-young-people-in-england/2020-wave-1-follow-up

Thandi, S (2020b) *Mental Health of Children and Young People in England, 2020: Wave 2 Follow Up to the 2017 Survey*. Available online at: https://digital.nhs.uk/data-and-information/publications/statistical/mental-health-of-children-and-young-people-in-england/2021-follow-up-to-the-2017-survey/copyright

The Association of Directors of Children's Services Ltd (2021) *Safeguarding Pressures Phase 7*. Available online at: https://adcs.org.uk/assets/documentation//ADCS_Safeguarding_Pressures_Phase7_FINAL.pdf

The Child Poverty Act (2010) Great Britain. Available online at: https://www.legislation.gov.uk/ukpga/2010/9/contents

The Children and Young People's Mental Health Taskforce (2015) *Future in Mind: Promoting, Protecting and Improving Our Children and Young People's Mental Health and Wellbeing*. Available online at: https://webarchive.nationalarchives.gov.uk/ukgwa/20170505113443/https:/www.gov.uk/government/uploads/system/uploads/attachment_data/file/414024/Childrens_Mental_Health.pdf

The Children's Commissioner (2017) *Digital 5 a Day*. Available online at: https://www.childrenscommissioner.gov.uk/digital/5-a-day/

The Children's Commissioner (2018) *Life in Likes Report*. Available online at: https://www.childrens-commissioner.gov.uk/wp-content/uploads/2018/01/Childrens-Commissioner-for-England-Life-in-Likes-3.pdf

The Children's Commissioner (2019a) *Gaming the System*. Available online at: https://www.childrenscommissioner.gov.uk/wp-content/uploads/2019/10/CCO-Gaming-the-System-2019.pdf

The Children's Commissioner (2019b) *Statutory Duty of Care Owed by Online Service Providers to Children*. Available online at: https://cco-web.azureedge.net/wp-content/uploads/2019/02/cco-duty-of-care-owed-by-online-service-providers-to-children.pdf

The Children's Society (2021) *Good Childhood Report 2020*. Available online at: https://www.childrens-society.org.uk/good-childhood

The Mental Health Taskforce (2016) *The Five Year Forward View for Mental Health. A Report from the Independent Mental Health Taskforce to the NHS in England. February 2016*. Available online at: https://www.england.nhs.uk/wp-content/uploads/2016/02/Mental-Health-Taskforce-FYFV-final.pdf

Townsend, P (1979) *Poverty in the United Kingdom*. London: Allen Lane and Penguin Books.

Transport for London (2021) *Transport Accessibility*. Available online at: https://tfl.gov.uk/transport-accessibility/

Tucker, J (2018) *The Impact of Poverty on Child Health*. Available online at: https://www.rcpch.ac.uk/news-events/news/impact-poverty-child-health

UNICEF (1989) *United Nations Convention on the Rights of the Child*. London: UNICEF. Available online at: https://www.unicef.org.uk/what-we-do/un-convention-child-rights/

United Nations Department of Economic and Social Affairs (2021) *Sustainable Development Goals*. Available online at: https://sdgs.un.org/goals

United Nations Human Rights Office of the High Commissioner (2014) *Day of General Discussion: "Digital Media and Children's Rights" 12 September 2014*. Available online at: https://www.ohchr.org/EN/HRBodies/CRC/Pages/Discussion2014.aspx

Urban Health (2021) *Air Pollution and Children. Urban Air Pollution and Children's Health: From Pregnancy to Early Adolescence*. Available online at: https://urbanhealth.org.uk/insights/reports/air-pollution-and-children

Wismer Fries, A and Pollak, S (2016) The role of learning in social development: Illustrations from neglected children. *Developmental Science*. Available online at: https://onlinelibrary.wiley.com/doi/10.1111/desc.12431

World Health Organisation (2008) *Closing the Gap in a Generation: Health Equity Through Action on the Social Determinants of Health - Final Report of the Commission on Social Determinants of Health.* Available online at: https://www.who.int/publications/i/item/WHO-IER-CSDH-08.1

World Health Organisation (2017) *Determinants of Health.* Available online at: https://www.who.int/newsroom/q-a-detail/determinants-of-health

Young Minds (2018). In **Bush, M** (ed), *Addressing Adversity: Prioritising Adversity and Trauma-Informed Care for Children and Young People in England.* Available online at: https://www.youngminds.org.uk/media/cmtffcce/ym-addressing-adversity-book-web-2.pdf

Index

A

Absolute poverty, 32, 33, 80
Adverse childhood experiences (ACEs), 2, 4, 16–18, 101
Advertising Standards Authority (ASA), 73
Affordable sports club, 81
Aggression, 49
Alzheimer's disease, 61
Anxiety, 2, 45, 49
Attainment gap, working families, 36–38, 79
Attention deficit hyperactive disorder (ADHD), 45, 49, 97
Autism, 25, 47, 49

B

Bailey, R., 70, 71, 74
Behavioural disorders, 47
Behaviour change, 51
Bioecological Model. *See* Ecological Systems Model
Black and minority ethnic (BAME) communities, 35, 44, 47, 79–80, 83, 85
Body Mass Index (BMI), 60
British Board of Film Classification (BBFC), 73
Bronfenbrenner, U., 3–4, 6, 12–15, 13 (figure), 61, 76, 87, 101–102, 105
Brown, C., 69
Byron, T., 67, 69, 70

C

Change4Life public health campaign, 26–27, 58, 64
Changing Places campaign, 96
Charities, 4, 19, 28, 30, 39–40, 51, 52, 91, 102
Child and Adolescent Mental Health Service (CAMHS), 49–50
Child carers, 98
Childcare tax credit, 34
Child Food Poverty, 63
Child Poverty Action Group, 31
Children Act, 15, 17, 31
Children and Young People's Mental Health Service (CYPMHS), 12, 49–50
Chronosystem, 15
Civic sector, health promotion, 28
Climate change, 78–79
Climbié, Victoria, 15
Cognitive development, 46, 58
Conduct disorders, 45
COVID-19 pandemic, 3, 5, 8, 9, 15, 19, 20, 23–24, 40–41, 46, 48, 52, 60–62, 66–67, 69, 79, 83–85, 87, 90, 91, 96, 100
Czerniewicz, L., 69

D

'5 a Day' campaign, 26, 55–56, 64, 75, 75 (figure)
Deep-level learning, 48
Dementia, 61
Department for Work and Pensions, 33, 40, 93
Department of Health and Social Care, 57
Depression, 2, 45, 49, 61
Development and Wellbeing Assessment tool, 47
DiClemente, C.C., 24
Dietary reference values, 56, 59
Diets. *See* Nutrition
Digital access scheme, 41
Digital divide, 41, 75
Digital Economy Act, 74
Digital immigrants, 69
Digital media, 6, 66, 104
    4G networks, 66–67
    and children's rights, 67–68
    contemporary discourse, 70
    self-isolation rules, 70
    social lives, 71–72
Digital Natives, 69, 70
Digital poverty, 40–41, 67, 77
Digital resilience, 74–76, 75 (figure)
Disability employment gap, 93
Disability Living Allowance (DLA), 92
Disabled Children's Partnership (DCP), 90
Disney, 72
Duffy, M., 31

E

Early Intervention Foundation, 87
Early Years community, 47, 49
Early Years Foundation Stage (EYFS), 75
Eating disorders, 47
Ecological Systems Model, 3–4, 6, 12, 29, 61, 76–77, 101–102, 105
    child development theory, 13
    exosystem, 14
    macrosystem, 14–15
    mesosystem, 13, 14
    microsystem, 13, 14
    nested structure, 13, 13 (figure)
Education, Health and Care Plan, 94
Emotional disorders, 47
Emotional wellbeing, 54, 100, 106
End Child Poverty Coalition, 34, 38–40
Environmental influences, 7
    educational needs and disabilities, 84
    health and education, 80
    'nature *vs.* nurture' debate, 78
    parenting style, 86–87

parents' wellbeing, 85–86
postcode lottery, of childhood experience, 78–80
rural *vs.* urban childhoods, 80–84
uncertain employment, 80
Equality Act, 89, 95
Estimated Average Requirements (EAR), 56
Ethnicity pay gap, 35
EU Kids Online Project, 70, 71, 75
Every Child Matters, 15
Exercise, 61–62
Exosystem, 14

F
Faith groups, 40
Family Resources Survey, 33
Field, F., 21, 31
Financial inequalities, 102
Financial management, 4
Five Year Forward View for Mental Health, 45, 46
Folic acid supplementation, 59
Food bank system, 40, 42
The Foundation Years, 21, 31
Future in Mind report, 49

G
Gender pay gap, 35
General Data Protection Regulations (GDPR), 68, 76
Geographical inequalities, 38–39
George, Alex, 52
Glanz, K., 23
Good Childhood report, 28, 74
Government-funded health promotion campaigns, 26, 27
Government policy, 1–7, 10, 19, 21, 29, 47, 64, 94, 106
nutrition deficiencies, 11
policy intervention, 12
position, 35–37
poverty, 11
Greta Thunberg Effect, 71

H
Health belief model, 51
action stage, 24, 26
addictive behaviours, 24
categories, 22–23
change model, 24, 24 (figure), 26, 27
contemplation stage, 24, 26, 27
cues to action, 23, 26
individual perceptions, 23
likelihood of action, 23
modifying factors, 23, 26
pre-contemplation stage, 24, 26, 27
preparation/decision stage, 24, 26
processes of change stage, 24
relapse zone, 24–25

Health damaging behaviours, 16
Health determinants, 1, 3–5, 8, 19, 27, 29, 30, 43, 54, 66, 78, 100–102, 103
adverse childhood experiences (ACEs), 16–18
children's commissioners role, 12–15, 12 (figure), 19
education and training, 9
within families, 18
government policy, 10–12
health needs, 19
obesity, 10
policy agendas, 10
postcode lottery, childhood experience, 10
wellbeing, 15–16
Health-harming behaviours, 2
Health inequalities, 7, 30, 82, 83, 90
family life, 105–106
Health promotion, 1, 2, 4, 6, 18, 19, 20–22, 25, 29, 51, 53, 58, 102, 106
and parenting, 26–28
right audience, 101
third sector, 28–29
Healthy Child Programme, 10, 26–27, 58
Healthy Child Programme 0–5 years, 21, 79
Healthy Child Programme 0–19, 22
Healthy Start Scheme, low-income families, 57
Holiday Activities and Food Programme, 62
Hospital/peripatetic education, 95–96
Hyperactivity disorders, 47

I
Independent sector, health promotion, 28
Individual poverty, 34–35
Innocence *vs.* knowledge, 6
Institute of Health Equity, 82
Intergenerational social mobility, 37
In-work poverty, 34, 41, 42, 81
Iron deficiency anaemia, 59

J
Joseph Rowntree Foundation, 11, 32, 33, 34, 40

K
Kwashiorkor, 55

L
Labour Sure Start policies, 87
Laevers, F., 48
Learning loss, 79
Leuven Scales, 48
Lewis, O., 34–35
Life in Likes report, 71–72, 74, 76
Local Authority Children's Services, 85, 87
Longfield, Anne, 71
Lower Reference Nutrient Intakes (LRNI), 56

M

Macronutrients, 56

Macrosystem, 6, 14–15, 29, 31, 36, 61, 62, 87, 100–102, 105

Malnutrition, 55–56

Marasmus, 55

Marmot, M., 7, 10, 21, 82, 84

McNeish, D., 31

Measles, Mumps and Rubella (MMR) vaccination, 25

Media, 6, 23, 62, 76. *See also* Digital media; Social media

  activities and content, 73–74

  children's rights, 67–68

  intertextuality, 72, 73, 104

  technology-enhanced learning, 75

  use of, 68–71

Mental health conditions and disorders, 51, 76, 100

  cognitive development, 46

  marginalisation, 45

  in older age, 46–47

  pre-school children, 47

  psychological therapy, 45

  stigmatisation, 45

Mental Health in Education Action Group, 52

Mental health issues, 5, 8, 9, 31, 101, 102–103

  behaviour change, 51

  Child and Adolescent Mental Health Service (CAMHS), 49–50

  Children and Young People's Mental Health Service (CYPMHS), 49–50

  COVID-19 pandemic, 48

  employment and education, 45

  Future in Mind report, 49

  good and poor wellbeing, 44

  health conditions and disorders, 45–47

  NHS Long Term Plan, 43

  No Health Without Mental Health, 44–45

  online community, 51

  social media, 51

  stigmatisation, 51

  third sector and influencers, 52

  time to change, 51

  wellbeing, in early years, 48–49

  Young Minds, 52

Mental Health of Children and Young People, 46

Mental health promotion, 43

Mental health services, 3, 43, 46

Mesosystem, 13, 14, 62, 105

Micronutrients, 56

Microsystem, 6, 7, 13, 14, 30, 31, 61, 62, 78, 86, 87, 100

Millennial generation, 69

MMR vaccination. *See* Measles, Mumps and Rubella (MMR) vaccination

N

National Child Measurement Programme, 6, 10, 11, 59, 60, 62

National Diet and Nutrition Survey, 55–56, 58, 59

National Disability Strategy, 93, 95

National Health Service (NHS), 2, 20

  healthy lifestyles, 21

National Portage Association Stamp of Approval, 94

NHS Long Term Plan, 1, 47, 49, 50

  parity of esteem, 11, 43, 49

Nintendo, 72

Non-government organisations, 4, 19, 58

NSPCC 'Full Stop' campaign, 28

Nursery Milk Scheme, 57

Nutrition, 5–6, 8, 9, 18, 27. *See also* Malnutrition

  childhood obesity, 59–61

  children's diets, 54, 56, 62

  deficiencies, 11, 58–59

  emotional wellbeing, 54

  and exercise, 61–62

  government policies and initiatives, 55

  government support, in young children, 57–58

  over-nutrition, 5, 58–59

  poor nutrition, 5

  sustainable childhoods, 103

  third sector, 62–64

  under-nutrition, 58–59

O

Obesity, 5–6, 10, 21, 27, 58, 59–61, 70, 103

Ofcom, 71, 74

Oliver, Jamie, 62, 63

Opportunity Areas programme, 37

Organisation for Economic Co-operation and Development (OECD), 83

Over-nutrition, 58–59

P

Pan European Games Information (PEGI), 73

Parental attitudes, 6

Parental responsibility, 30–31

Parenting style, 86–87

Pauperism, 34. *See also* Absolute poverty

Personal Independence Payment (PIP), 92

Physical/genetic conditions, 7

  child carers, 98

  child health outcomes, 89

  Coronavirus Act, 91

  disability and health conditions, 95

  Disabled Children's Partnership (DCP), 90

  family life, disability impact, 91–93, 98–99

  financial considerations, 93–94

  health care services, 92

  health inequalities, 90

  hospital/peripatetic education, 95–96

Local Authority, 98
medical model of, 99
play therapy, 95–96
portage, 94–95
reasonable endeavours, 91
self-care, 91
self-esteem, 92
services access, 96–98
social distancing, 91
social model, 90
working families, 94
Physical health services, 3
Play therapy, 95–96
Pokémon card game, 72
Postcode lottery, of childhood experience, 1, 5,
10, 38, 78–80, 84, 85, 104–105
Postman, N., 68
Post-traumatic stress, 2
Poverty, 4–5, 8, 9, 11, 59
absolute, 32
attainment gap, 37–38
'cared for,' 30–31
causes of, 32
childcare and disability, 40
Coalition Government, 32
COVID-19 pandemic, 40–41
culture of, 5, 34–35
definition, 32
diets and nutrition, 6, 9
digital, 40–41, 67, 77
environmental influences, 30
essential items, 33
family and genetic issues, 30
food bank system, 40, 42
geographical inequalities, 38–39
government policy position, 35–37
health conditions, 31
individual lifestyle, 30
individual poverty, 34–35
infant mortality, 31
in-work, 34, 41, 42, 81
line, 39, 102
measurements and indicators, 33
persistance and causes, 34
poverty line, 33
relative, 32, 33, 34, 80
resources, 40
risky behaviours, 31
social exclusion, 32
social factors, 30
Social Metrics Commission, 40, 41
social mobility, 37–38
socio-economic risks, 31
structural poverty, 34, 35
third sector organisations, 33, 39–42
working, 38, 64, 102, 103

Prochaska, J.O., 24
Psychosis, 45–46, 47
Public Health England, 58–61
Public health issues, 4, 20
childhood vaccinations and screenings, 21
health and risk behaviours, 22
health belief model, 22–25, 24 (figure)
healthy parenting choices, 26–27
in sustainable childhoods, 21–22
UK child immunisation programme, 25
welfare benefit system, 21

R
Rashford, Marcus, 36, 62, 63, 103
Reference Nutrient Intakes (RNI), 56
Relative poverty, 32, 33, 34, 80
Resilience, 48
Risk-taking behaviours, 3

S
Savage, M., 75
School Food Plan, 18, 58
School Food Regulations, 58
School Food Standards, 61–62
School Fruit and Vegetable Scheme, 57
School Sport and Activity Plan, 61
Screen-based activities, 74
Selective mutism, 47
Self-care, 49, 91
Self-esteem, 48, 92
Self-harm, 71, 76
Self-isolation rules, 70
Self-professed strategy, 44
Social activism, 71
Social inequalities, 1, 83
Social isolation, 81, 82
Social justice, 40, 44
Social media, 51, 52, 68, 76
Social Metrics Commission, 40, 41, 96
Social Metrics Measure, 93
Social mobility, 37–38, 82
Solihull Approach, 87
Special Educational Needs (SEN), 95
Special Educational Needs and Disabilities
(SEND), 94–95
Start4Life programme, 87
Statutory Duty of Care for Online Service
Providers, 76
Stern, D., 86
Strengths and Difficulties Questionnaire (SDQ),
48
Structural inequalities, 35
Structural poverty, 34, 35
Supporting Families Programme, 87
Sustainable Development Goals, 78, 79, 81,
104–105

T
Tax credit system, 32, 34, 35
Third sector organisations, poverty, 33, 39–42
Thunberg, Greta, 71
Trade unions, 40
Triple P, 87
Troubled Families Programme, 87
Trussell Trust, 36, 41–42, 102

U
UK child immunisation programme, 25
UK Physical Activity Guidelines, 61
Under-nutrition, 58–59
United Nations Convention on the Rights of the Child (UNCRC), 3, 10, 12, 35, 67
Universal Credit, 34
Universal free school meal, 11, 18, 33, 35, 36, 38, 39, 57, 62, 63, 85, 103

V
Vitamin C deficiency, 55, 59
Vitamin D deficiency, 55, 58–59
Voluntary organisations, 4, 19
Voluntary sector, health promotion, 28

W
Wakefield, Andrew, 25
Welfare benefit system, 21, 32, 34, 35, 47, 84, 102, 106
Welfare Food Regulations, 57
Welfare organisations, 40
Welfare Reform and Work Act, 36
Working poverty, 36, 38, 64, 102, 103

Y
Young Minds, 52